Certifying Your

Facilities

Maintenance Program

Class A

By Steve Hampson

ISBN 978-0-6152-0318-8

Table of Contents

Plant Data Structure
- Plant equipment and/or location structure
- Bills of Material (BOMs)
- Pre-planned maintenance tasks
- Work centers
- Authorization documents
- Special skills
- Change management process

Maintenance Programs
- Preventative (PM)
- Autonomous (AM)
- Reactive and condition-based (RM & CBM)
- Backlogs

Maintenance Planning and Execution
- Planning, scheduling, and capacity utilization
- Priority systems
- Performing the work
- Reporting
- Budgeting

Material Planning
- Output of planning systems and ability to meet needs
- Supplier involvement
- Stock usage, safety stock, leveraged purchasing
- Parts inventory process
- Parts delivery process (to work area)

Measures
- Success Measures
- Data analysis & continuous improvement

Organizational Effectiveness
- Organizational structure
- Specific maintenance philosophies
- Computer systems

Welcome from the Author

Welcome to <u>Certifying Your Maintenance Program as Class A.</u>

The goal of this book is to help structure a Class A maintenance process based on planning, not reactive maintenance, which maximizes the efficiency of resources and provides <u>significant</u> savings.

The 470 question checklist inside looks at every aspect of a maintenance program and asks in-depth questions about how each process is designed and executed. A point value is assigned to each answer and a cumulative score earned. That score will identify strengths and weaknesses in your maintenance programs, as well as determine what areas are eligible for certification.

Ideally, once your maintenance program is certified Class A, your people will spend most of their time managing the planning parameters and doing continuous improvement projects, rather than resolving near-term problems.

The goal is to help companies determine the best level of planning for their business and provide a framework to get them there. This book will provide you with the guidelines on how to start down the road towards those areas in need of improvement. Ultimately, this book will help you realize savings through:

- Better resource usage
- Spare part inventory reductions
- Leveraged material and service purchasing
- Increased productivity of people and machines
- Improved documentation for data analysis and continuous improvement

The unique aspect of this book is there are no other in-depth audit and/or certification programs for maintenance. This book is the first its kind.

Best of luck with your program and I hope you are able to learn something useful in your audit.

Steve Hampson

Note: If you need an independent audit or additional information on how to use your results, you may contact the author at info@classamaintenance.com or see the website www.classamaintenance.com.

Introduction

For many years, manufacturing industries have been driven by a sales-first approach, followed closely by production. Employee training is usually the only element lower on the totem pole than maintenance. In recent years the tide has begun to turn in some companies, but only very slowly and often with little real commitment to involving maintenance in the overall planning and execution processes.

It is clear to see why maintenance is important. It controls the overall operability of the plant equipment, its success determines the amount of planned and unplanned downtime in the production processes, and it can have a very significant impact on the bottom-line costs of the product.

However, maintenance work still takes a back seat to these other areas when it is time to make tough decisions. "We must generate sales to make a product," is the corporate norm and let the next manager figure out how to recover from the results of putting off maintenance events. Instead, I argue, what should happen is that each department should meet on an even playing field and decisions made based on data which take into account the short and long-term impacts of each option.

That is where a Class A maintenance program comes in.

A best-in-class or Class A maintenance program is truly integrated throughout the different aspects of your business. Typically, that means sales, purchasing, production, infrastructure support (which includes training and IT), finance, and maintenance (in no particular order). The requirements of each of these areas are very important to the individual business areas. However, the best companies take into account how their decisions impact on each different area and involve them in the decision-making process.

Several programs already exist to evaluate the performance of most of the individual elements of a business. The Class A maintenance audit program examines the internal work processes of a maintenance department and how they interact with the other areas of your company. Each question in this audit program is designed to determine how the processes are executed within your company and assigns a point value to their efficiency. That point value has been established from examining best practice for carrying out a specific task within the maintenance process, regardless of the industry. The resultant grade determines how well your plant performs that task and will open doors to improvement as necessary.

The ultimate goal of any improvement program is to provide opportunities for cost savings. Maintenance is the last area of business where big money can be saved in the manufacturing process. The maintenance concepts in this book relate directly to cost reduction and will lead you towards solutions that will support the following:

- Maintenance programs based on planning, not reactive maintenance, and which share data with other aspects of your business
- Streamlining the parts supply process, including reducing inventories and leveraged purchasing
- Using an aggressive continuous improvement program
- Reduced downtime owing to
  - planning downtime, not being reactive
  - continuous improvements for less unplanned downtime
  - maximize downtime efficiency
- Streamlined processes for production, maintenance, and purchasing

What I would encourage you to do is to approach this audit with an open mind and a willingness to learn new approaches. Just because it has always been done a certain way does not mean that it is still the best way. And, if it is, it still needs to be documented and shared with others in your department, plant and even company.

This audit is very comprehensive and should be undertaken over the course of at least a week. If performed internally, I recommend the creation of an objective team of managers who have extensive experience and ability in the areas they will review. The audit should be led by a department head and sponsored by a director or plant manager. For the best possible results, it is not recommended that managers audit their own personnel or work processes. After the results are generated, it is best that the managers sit together and discuss them. Not only to identify the areas of improvements and verify that the results are true, but also to prioritize the issues that are discovered and come up with a plan to develop solutions for each problem area over a pre-determined period of time. Finally, a second audit to status-check the progress of the identified areas of improvement should be conducted within 3-4 months of the initial audit.

Alternatively, you can have an external maintenance expert or consultant perform the audit. For timing estimates, a complete review should take one person 7-10 business days, with another 5 days for a complete report with recommendations on improvements, etc. That is the standard a company should expect from external auditors.

This audit program will look specifically into the following aspects of the maintenance business and how they relate to the rest of the departments in your plant:

- Plant data structure
- Maintenance programs
- Maintenance planning and execution
- Material planning
- Organizational effectiveness
- Measures

Each aspect of the maintenance business is broken down into several sub-areas. Depending on the answers to the questions, a grade based on a 4.0 scale will be assigned to each sub area, as well as the overall process, and then the maintenance business as a whole. From there, you can review the next steps section to start down the road to improvement and savings.

This book will start with a description of best practice for each maintenance area. Given a clean slate, how could a Class A maintenance program be established? The 470 question audit follows. By the end of your audit, hopefully you will have learned a great deal and paid for this book within 15 minutes of implementing your first improvement.

Why is Maintenance Important?

So why do maintenance? Well like anything else, money is the prime motivating factor. No one goes into business to lose money, regardless of how benevolent the good or service is that they provide. Capital investment is a large part of the start-up costs of any company and maintenance is a good way to make sure that investment makes the best possible return for the longest possible time.

Once a business has been operating for a while, it has to start balancing priorities. Its ability to sell and deliver on that sale (production) becomes the driving factor in the daily life of a manager because it most visibly impacts the bottom line. What can often be overlooked is how maintenance costs also impact that bottom line. It can happen in several ways:

- The inability to make product because equipment is down
- Rising costs of parts inventory and labor raises overall overhead costs and cuts into profit margins
- Unperformed maintenance can reduce manufacturing efficiencies

Thus, a good maintenance program can have a significantly positive impact on a company's overall profitability.

An Integrated PM Program
Helps Achieve Two Goals
Which Will Lead to Significant
Business Savings

Graphic X-1

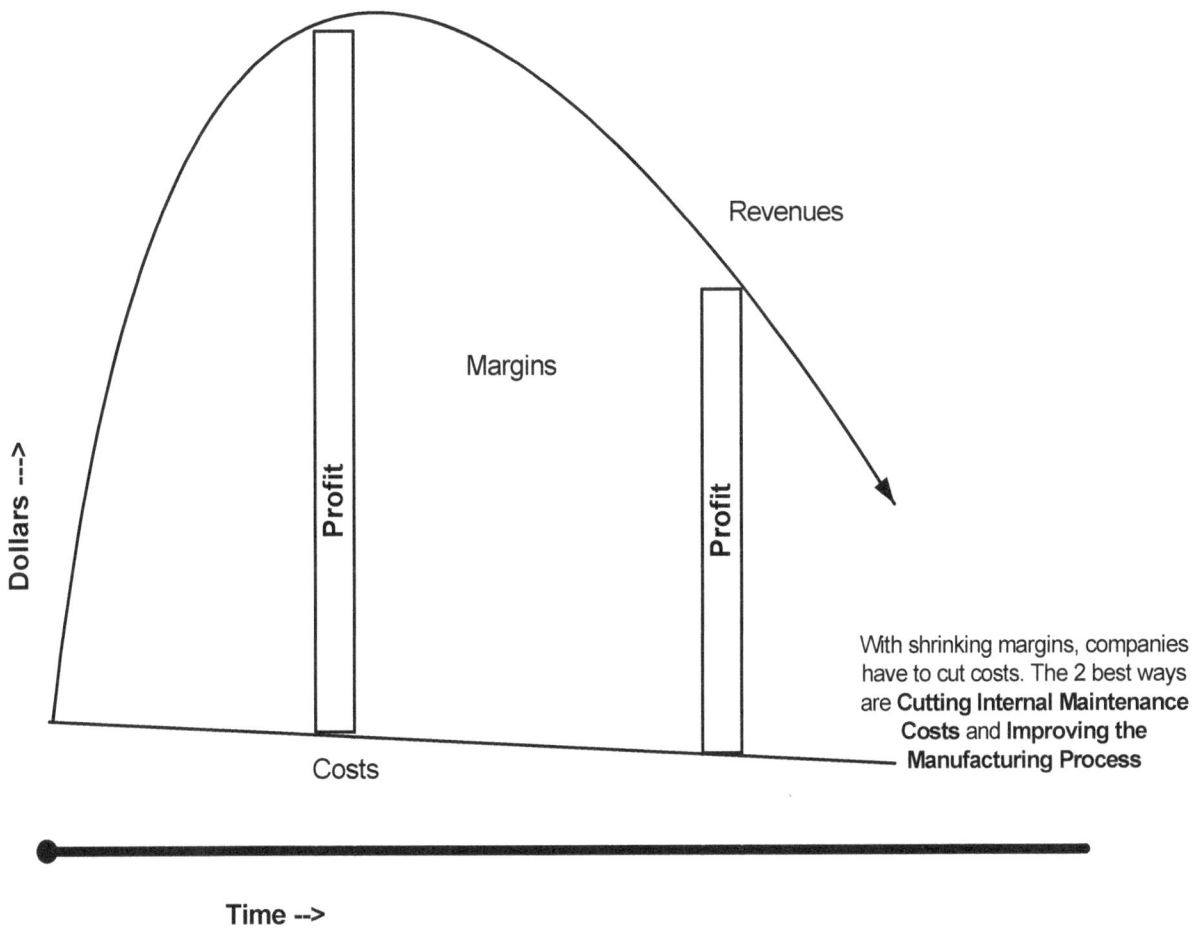

Revenues

Margins

Profit

Profit

Dollars --->

With shrinking margins, companies have to cut costs. The 2 best ways are **Cutting Internal Maintenance Costs** and **Improving the Manufacturing Process**

Costs

Time -->

Cutting Internal Maintenance Costs
and
Improving the Manufacturing Process

Graphic X-1 above shows that as revenues decline, companies have to cut costs to keep profit margins up. Investing in maintenance can help cut those maintenance costs and lead to improved manufacturing processes. This provides two steps of improvement (efficiency up, overhead down) for one effort.

A maintenance program which is certified Class A will deliver those kinds of results and can sustain them for the long-term. Class A maintenance processes are integrated with production and sales activity for a complete business view which allows for better decisions based on accurate and current data.

Specific benefits of a Class A certified maintenance program include:

Cut Internal Maintenance Costs

- Identify opportunities for optimizing maintenance execution
- Justify expenditures for predictive maintenance technologies
- Optimize spare parts inventory to minimize inventory costs and bring "maverick inventories" under control
- Optimize maintenance resource utilization
- One data source for all maintenance information including a hierarchy of all plant equipment with serialization history
- Automatically generate a purchase request and link to the order needing the service or part
- Reduced overtime through better planning
- Web-enable some or all of data and functions for both technicians and internal customers
- Standardized business processes across all maintenance areas, leveraging improvements and geometrically increasing savings across the plant or multiple plants
- Dispatching of resources with specific problem information based on a priority system

Improving the Manufacturing Process

- Improved manufacturing up-time
- Increased asset life
- Improved ability to troubleshoot
- Justify asset overhaul or replacement if needed
- Identify maintenance opportunities to improve performance
- Capture equipment performance data
- Objective maintenance prioritization systems

- Results in a completely integrated production and maintenance plan where maintenance downtime can be planned at the S&OP level

The goal of a Class A Maintenance program is to totally change the maintenance rewards system.

Your best preventative maintenance "Maytag repairman" should always be more recognized than your best corrective maintenance "Firefighter." To do that, each company has to make the maintenance department part of the team that runs the overall company. As part of that team, the maintenance department must be committed to develop a maintenance solution that efficiently operates the 6 links in the maintenance business chain. (see figure X-2 below)

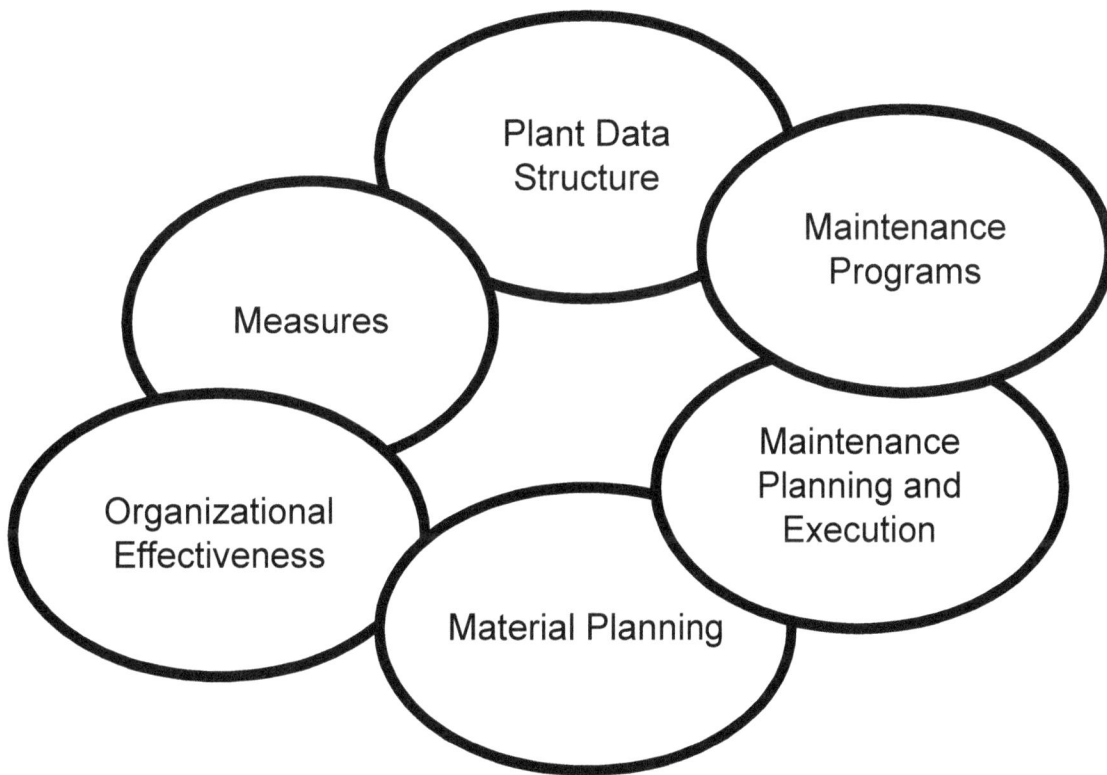

This book will take a maintenance manager through the Best Practice and audit requirements to achieve those goals and get to those savings. Once a Class A maintenance program is in place, the maintenance manager can monitor the maintenance parameters and execute the plan, thereby making them a real life "Maytag Repairman."

Maintenance Best Practices

In an attempt to define what a Class A maintenance program is, each link in the maintenance business chain can be broken into its key Best Practice areas. Each key area is important for the reasons described in this chapter. Descriptions and a Class A example are provided below.

Each section is written from a perspective of, "If I could start a maintenance department from scratch, how would it look?" Few readers of this book can really do this, but hopefully these Best Practices can be goals for maintenance managers to strive to meet or exceed, with the help of the following audit and suggestions for improvement chapters.

By at least meeting the standards set forth in these Best Practices, Class A status can be achieved.

Plant Data Structure

Purpose

Creating a database of plant maintenance information provides an essential resource which can be used for several facets of a maintenance program. Obviously, the more robust and accurate the information in the database, the better the chance one will have to identify areas for improvement.

However, one cannot stress enough the importance of creating a good Plant Data Structure and accurately maintaining it.

Using this data, analysis is performed and decisions are made. The better the data structure and more accurate the data, the more likely the decisions made will be correct and maximize the savings achieved.

Thus, the seven key areas of every maintenance database are:

Plant equipment	A record created for a piece of equipment within a plant.
Bills of Material (BOMs)	A group of materials which make up a specific object or are required for a task.
Pre-planned maintenance tasks	A pre-defined template that can be pulled into a work order or maintenance plan that identifies the work to be conducted, the components needed, the estimated effort required, the frequency of the task, the external resources needed, and any external documents to be used for the task.
Work centers	Groups responsible for performing the maintenance work. Can be grouped by any variable including cost center, special skills, line or process, etc.
Authorization documents	Documents that are required for approval in order to begin, execute, or end a maintenance task.
Special skills	The technical ability or aptitude of the person required to complete a task.
Change management process	The process to maintain the accuracy of maintenance records in order to reflect current plant structure, record production activity, maintenance events, item performance and cost history.

The establishment of each key item is imperative to the success of the maintenance database. Every IT person will tell you "Garbage in = Garbage out." The same is true for a maintenance database.

The foundation of every Class A certified maintenance program is a sound maintenance database which is complete and accurate. It is the basis for all other advancements and improvements in the maintenance business.

Key Best Practice areas:

- **Plant equipment and/or location structure**

<u>Why it is important:</u>

Every maintenance manager should have a set of records for the equipment in their plant. Creating these records allows for tracking maintenance repair and cost history that occurs at a specific, stationary location and/or specific serialized asset throughout its life. Should a separate equipment record be generated for objects that change place throughout a plant, its movement history can be tracked while the maintenance and cost history goes with the object. With a well-known location structure in place, maintenance work can be written to dispatch a technician to a specific work location. A plant location and equipment hierarchy can be represented in a Graphical Information System GIS system to help with problem reporting and asset tracking. Serialized asset records would be assigned to each location. A plant hierarchy is built to map the facility and track asset location and movement. This location and equipment hierarchy is the first piece of any life cycle tracking and data analysis program as it provides for excellent asset matching and benchmarking capability.

<u>Plant Hierarchy Example:</u>

<u>1st Level</u>   Business and plant

     Ex: CBDC   Circuit Boards, Decatur
         BTDC   Battery Charging, Decatur
         CBCN   Circuit Boards, Cincinnati

2nd <u>Level</u>   Line or process

     Ex: CBDC-0001   Circuit Boards, Line 1
         BTDC-0003   Battery Charging, Line 3

<u>3rd Level</u>   Unit operation/Major equipment

Ex: CBDC-0002-0100   Surface Mount
     BTCN-0010-0400   Coil Winding

(At this level and lower levels, BOMs, Equipments, Assemblies and their BOMs may start to be attached.)

<u>4th Level</u>   Identifies a subarea or major assembly of the production line or system

Ex: CBDC-0001-0100-0040   Oven
     CBDC-0004-0200-0020   Axial Inserter

<u>5th Level</u>   Identifies a component or sub-assembly within the unit operation.

Ex: CBCN-0005-0100-0200-0020   Shelf mount conveyor
    CBDC-0002-0300-0020-0010   Wave solder flux addition

<u>6th level</u>   Identifies a component or sub-assembly within the unit operation or assembly

Ex: CBCN-0002-0200-0010-0010-0020   Board feeder carriage
    CBDC-0003-0100-0020-0070-0010   Shelf mount exhaust fan blade
                                        Assembly

Equipment Example:

Note: Separate from asset record, but can be linked to one to show where the specific equipment is

SN # 122   Pick & place shelf mount
    SN # 144   Drive motor   (sub equipment)
        402435 (SN)   Drive assembly
                       213443897 (PN)   Drive shaft   (component)
                       332444898   Drive gear   (component)
                       777719953   Lube oil   (component)
        402238   Computer assembly   (assembly in equipment)
        420005   Slide assembly   (assembly in equipment)
                       500004534   Housing   (component)
                       534459911   Rotor   (component)
                       211184992   Cooling water   (component)

13

- **Bills of Material (BOMs)**

.

<u>Why it is important:</u>

A Bill of Material serves two very useful purposes for a maintenance department. Firstly, it is a standardized parts list which can be use to identify assembly configuration, order replacements, stock maintenance storerooms, and identify no longer used parts inventories.

Secondly, a BOM can be a standardized list of parts, documents, drawings, etc for use in a maintenance event. This type of BOM helps technicians get the right set of parts for each task and assists the maintenance storeroom with work order staging, material purchasing, and planning.

In both cases, these standardized parts lists will lead to significant time and costs savings in both the short and long-term and can significantly impact the bottom line of a company.

Equipment BOM example

SN # 212   Power supply

400000202	Rotor Assembly	(sub equipment and BOM)
	564235137	Rotor
	232199628	Windings
	238423326	Brushes
581128923	Housing	
700000022		Power supply drawing
900000233		Power supply tech document

Maintenance event BOM example

232199628	Valves QTY – 1
238423326	Lines QTY - 2
581128923	Gauge QTY- 1
651277843	Grease QTY – 2 oz
700002013	LP air system drawing (## for CAD drawing)
900000776	LP air system tech doc (## for Word document)

- **Pre-planned maintenance tasks**

Why it is important:

Pre-planned maintenance tasks contain standard approaches for all types of maintenance activity. A standard maintenance procedure which includes step-by-step instructions, tool and parts lists, drawings, schematics, and even photos and video – all to help a technician perform the maintenance event more efficiently and accurately each time.

In addition, the pre-planned maintenance task for Preventative Maintenance (PM) and Autonomous Maintenance (AM) can be replicated into a work order based on the frequency required for the PM and AM tasks. For RM and CBM work, the technician will be able to use standard procedures to solve emergent problems.

Thus, in all cases, the resultant work order will be better planned and prepared for the maintenance technician, thus giving them the best opportunity for success in the most cost-effective manner and will provide for better maintenance data collection for future analysis.

Data in a pre-planned maintenance task example

Description of task list		Work center performing work	
Item being repaired		Required condition of item when work starts	
Step by step description			
Work (effort hours – in tenths of hours)		Duration (clock time of job)	
## of people		## of times job is to be performed in the operation	
Special tools		Special skills	

Parts required (part numbers and quantities)			

- **Work centers**

Why it is important:

Work centers represent the organization of maintenance personnel. They can be divided by cost center, skill set, production line/process, etc. In addition, hierarchies can be created to show relationships where resources are shared and /or costs and capacity roll-up.

The biggest advantages of this key Best Practice area for maintenance managers are:

- Labor usage and availability for work assignment
- Shift planning both on-shift and scheduling across-shift assignments
- Capacity planning – for large and small scale jobs
- Track technician time and labor rates

These factors are extremely helpful to a maintenance manager when it comes time to make decisions around planning, scheduling, and staffing, and go a long way towards determining and justifying annual budget requirements. A good work center structure can also provide for good data analysis and significant savings through planning and work efficiency.

Data in a work center example

Description		Leader/planner	
Employees assigned		Skills sets of each employee	
Work hours and parameters		Total capacity	
Shared workload?		Duration (clock time of job)	
Labor rates			

Sample Maintenance Organizational Chart

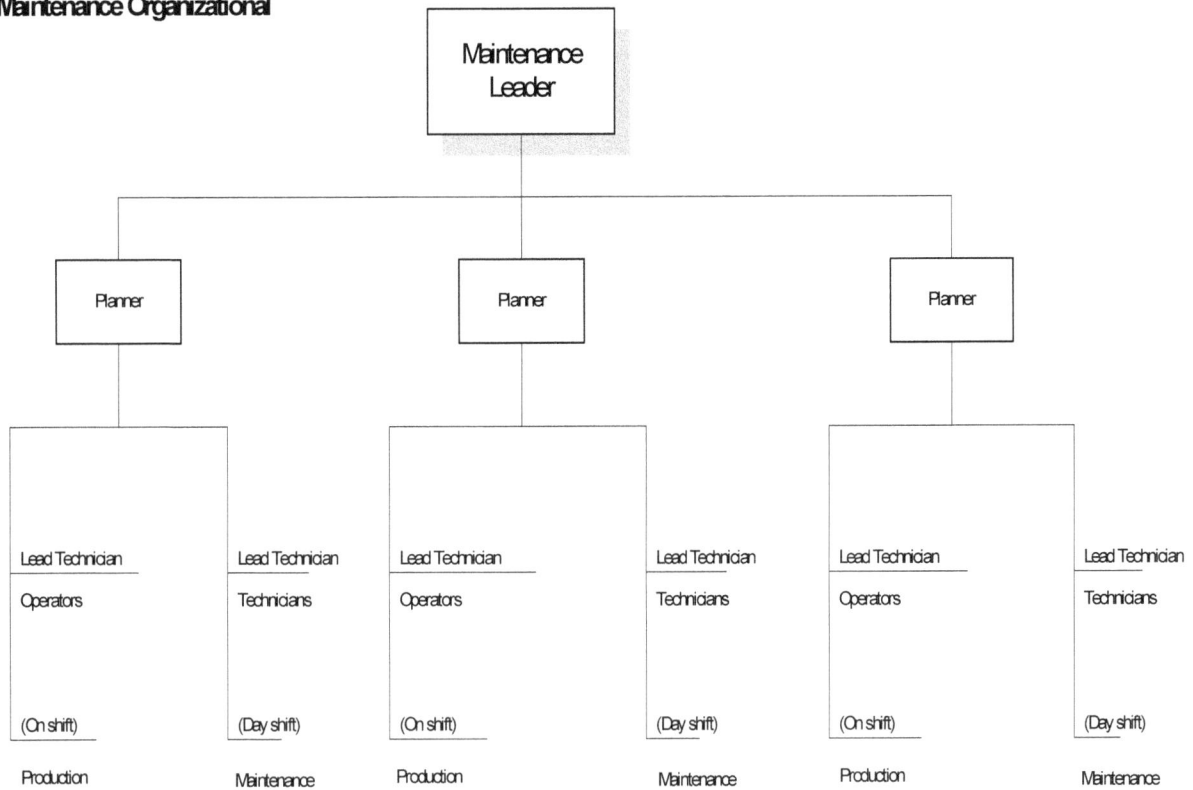

```
                          ┌──────────────┐
                          │  Maintenance │
                          │    Leader    │
                          └──────┬───────┘
           ┌─────────────────────┼─────────────────────┐
      ┌────┴────┐            ┌────┴────┐            ┌────┴────┐
      │ Planner │            │ Planner │            │ Planner │
      └────┬────┘            └────┬────┘            └────┬────┘
```

Lead Technician	Lead Technician	Lead Technician	Lead Technician	Lead Technician	Lead Technician
Operators	Technicians	Operators	Technicians	Operators	Technicians
(On shift)	(Day shift)	(On shift)	(Day shift)	(On shift)	(Day shift)
Production	Maintenance	Production	Maintenance	Production	Maintenance

- **Authorization documents**

<u>Why it is important:</u>

Many companies have maintenance tasks that require a certain level of approval in order to be started. These authorization documents detail the necessary steps to obtain the approval to start work. In most cases, the documents required are usually necessary to meet environmental, health, and safety concerns, but they can be used to notify production personnel of upcoming maintenance work and what effects the work may have on the process.

Another usage for authorization documents is to meet witnessing or QA certification requirements. These documents provide the opportunity to "sign off" the completion of the work and keep that approval with the rest of the maintenance records for a specific task.

Regardless of the usage, a standard format must be developed and implemented with a standard approval process. In most cases, the failure to complete this process properly will not only cause problems, but possibly cost lives.

The establishment of standardized authorization documents and the appropriate approval process is not only good maintenance business, it's good personnel safety business as well.

Authorization document example data:

Approver	The controlling body to which the request is submitted
Location	The location where the authorization is required
Applicant, work center, phone	The name, work group and phone number of the applicant
Authorization type	The type of authorization required
Start date/Time	The date and time when the event is to take place
End date/Time	The date and time when the event is to end
Equipment	A description of the equipment to be isolated
Work/Test	A description of the work/test to be completed
Hazards	A list of any known hazards in the work area
Authorization Request Number	Sequential authorization number

- **Special skills**

Why it is important:

Every maintenance manager should be able to identify the skill sets of their technicians under their control. Some may be able to assign a competency or proficiency level to that skill set.

By taking these steps and putting the results in a matrix, the maintenance planner can assign qualified technicians to the right work orders, thus making work execution more efficient.

In addition, by looking at upcoming skill requirements and the capacity to meet those skill requirements, maintenance managers can make good staff sizing decisions.

The bottom line is, better skill planning means better execution and additional opportunities in data analysis.

Matrix of skills and skill levels example

	Basic (B)	Advanced (A)	Expert (E)
Electrical (E)	EB	EA	EE
Plumbing (P)	PB	PA	PE
Pipefitting (F)	FB	FA	FE
Welding (W)	WB	WA	WE
Mechanical (M)	MB	MA	ME

- **Change management process**

<u>Why it is important:</u>

With all the plant data records to be created in a Class A maintenance program, there must be an efficient and consistent change management process in place or the data analysis will become meaningless in a short period of time.

Data integrity is critical to the proper functioning of the entire maintenance process. A rigid change management process should be in place to ensure that data integrity can be maintained. Generally, there are three types of changes that can be encountered. They are:

Routine in-plant changes	Equipment movements, configuration changes resulting from maintenance events, and other changes which may occur during the normal operation and maintenance of the business.
Project-related changes	When large scale projects alter plant configuration
User-requested changes	User recommendations for improvements of plant equipment or processes or to fix inaccuracies in the database

This process must be easily available, trained, and ingrained in all plant personnel. The importance of this can't be stressed enough. Decisions both large and small will be made from the analysis performed on the information in this plant database. To maximize the return on this effort the data must be as accurate as possible. This is one of the largest drivers of a maintenance manager's new work paradigm. In a Class A maintenance program, a maintenance manager spends more time on data analysis, managing parameters to book work efficiencies and lower costs, instead of putting out fires caused by unplanned production downtime and expediting necessary parts. An accurate database is one of the primary determining factors in the success of a maintenance analysis program

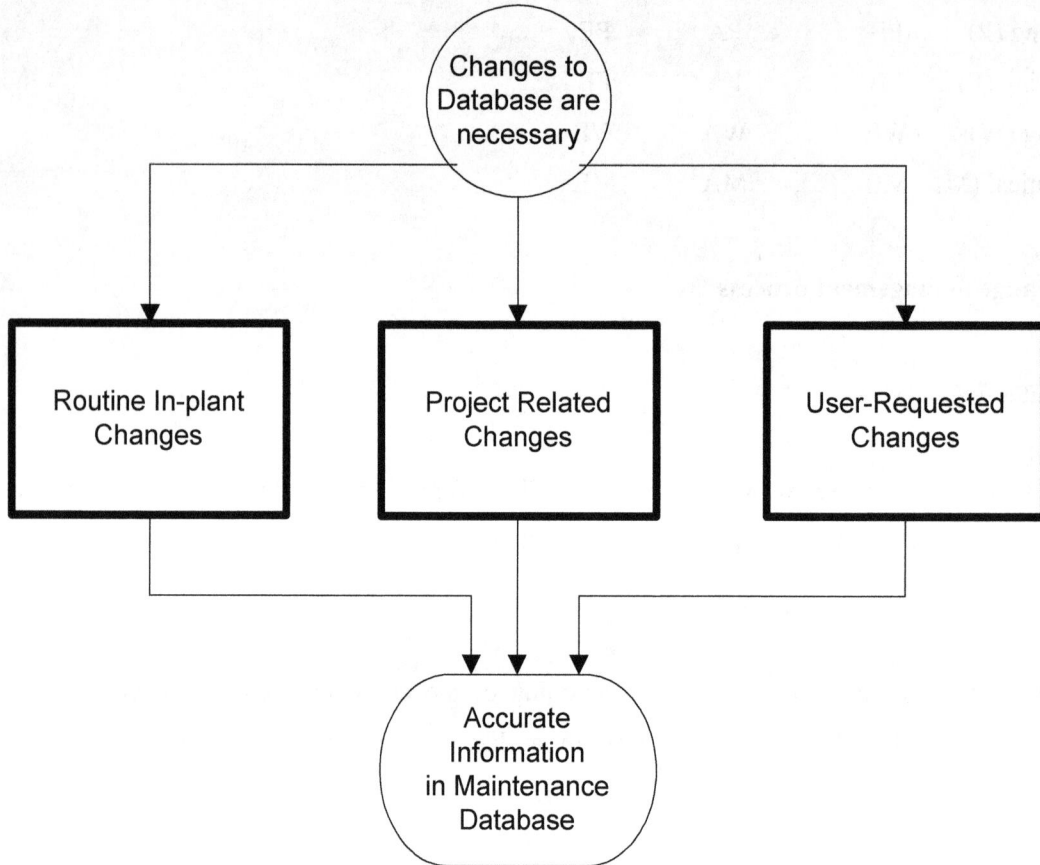

```
              ┌──────────────┐
              │  Changes to  │
              │ Database are │
              │  necessary   │
              └──────────────┘

┌─────────────┐  ┌─────────────┐  ┌─────────────┐
│ Routine In- │  │   Project   │  │    User-    │
│   plant     │  │   Related   │  │  Requested  │
│  Changes    │  │   Changes   │  │   Changes   │
└─────────────┘  └─────────────┘  └─────────────┘

              ┌──────────────┐
              │   Accurate   │
              │ Information   │
              │ in Maintenance│
              │  Database    │
              └──────────────┘
```

Maintenance Programs

Purpose

To identify and classify the types of maintenance performed in a company.

Maintenance work can be broken down into four significant areas. They are:

Preventative	A program consisting of a series of time and/or performance-based maintenance, it includes replacements, overhauls and major inspections which are essential to maintain optimal operating conditions
Autonomous	Equipment monitoring or basic maintenance requiring little or no downtime and only consumable components in order to keep the plant operating efficiently. Usually performed by operating personnel.
Reactive	All non-preventative maintenance work which emerges from day-to-day business operations. There are two types: 1) Emergency/breakdown - which directly affect reliability and must be corrected immediately 2) Planned - which permits time to plan and schedule the work into the integrated production/maintenance schedule. This work includes projects, business initiatives, safety items, and condition-based items which may involve maintenance resources
Backlog	List of outstanding tasks to be performed which do not have a specific completion data planned

The first three of these areas determine the entire maintenance worklist. The fourth area, the backlog, is usually a by-product of what is not completed from the maintenance worklist. How well these key Best Practice areas are formalized and documented is critical to the success of the maintenance department.

A maintenance department that relies on one complete work list with a backlog of pending and overdue work is reacting to the daily events of the business and therefore is not Class A. The best maintenance departments are those with formal programs which can be integrated into an overall maintenance plan that determines maintenance schedules and events and anticipates potential problems. These departments are much more efficient and fiscally successful.

Therefore, it is important that each plant has some kind of formal program for the three key Best Practice areas. Ideally, a Best-in-Class maintenance department does not have a backlog.

Maintenance Programs

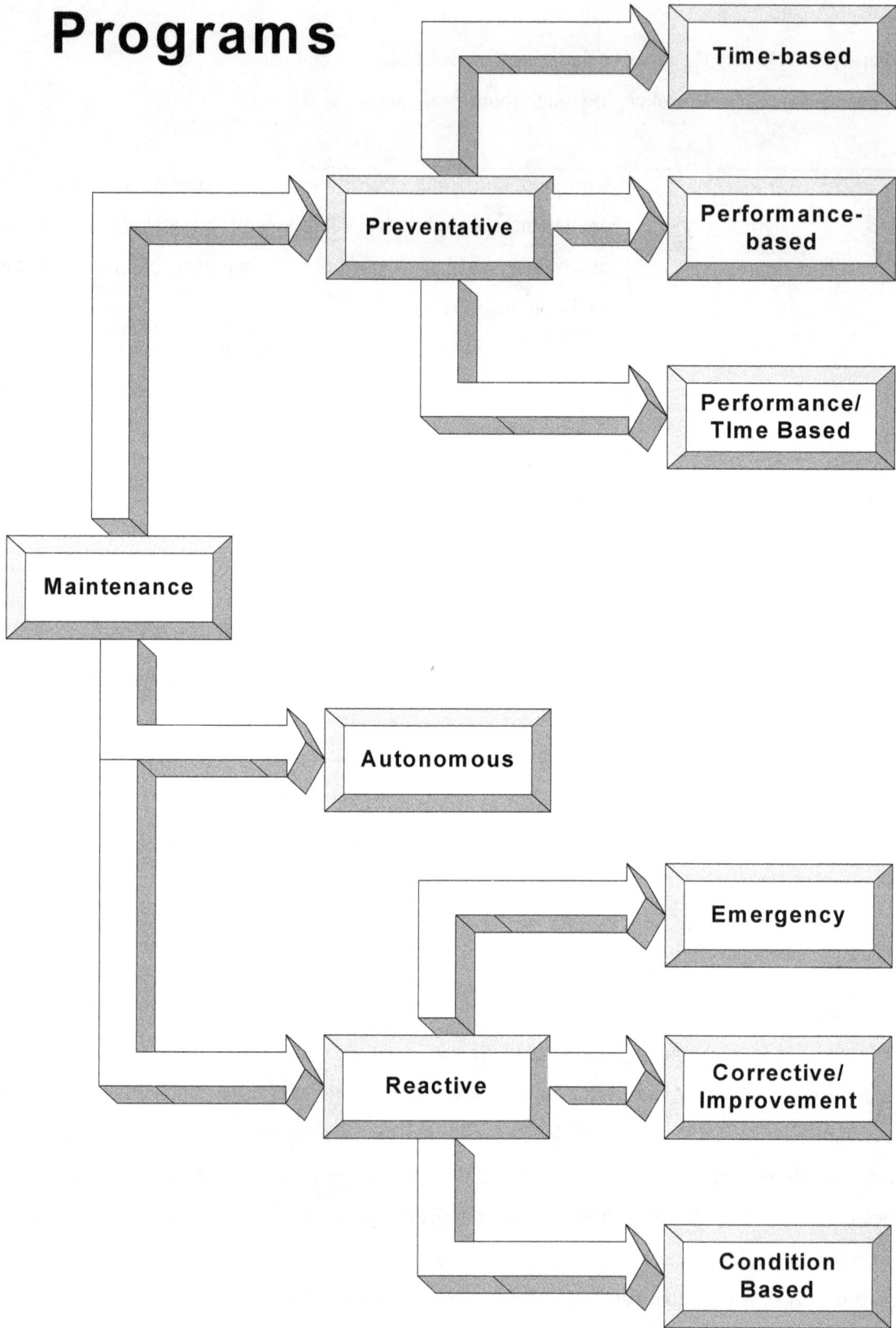

Time-based

Preventative

Performance-based

Performance/ TIme Based

Maintenance

Autonomous

Emergency

Reactive

Corrective/ Improvement

Condition Based

Key Best Practice areas:

- **Preventative (PM)**

<u>Why it is important:</u>

Every maintenance department has some type of preventative maintenance program. Some programs are executed better and more frequently than others, but their importance cannot be understated.

The goal of every PM program is to earn the largest and longest-term return on a company's capital investment in its production and support equipment.

Three are three levels of success in every PM Program. As each program moves up a level, their savings can increase geometrically.

The first level is having a PM program and executing it in a complete and consistent manner. With a PM program in place, the equipment will be getting regular attention and should perform better and more cost effectively.

The second level is doing the "right" PMs in a preventative maintenance program. In maintenance departments with a mature manufacturing process, generally 70% of the PMs in the program are really needed for the equipment. In addition, there are probably another 10% of PMs out there that have not been developed and which should be added to the existing PM program. A maintenance manager, through good data analysis, can determine which PMs provide the return on the investment of maintenance time and money. In addition, they can review reactive maintenance records to see if new PMs can be developed which can eliminate breakdowns and other unplanned maintenance events before they happen. A key element of this data analysis is the consistent execution of existing maintenance programs. If the in-place PM program is not carried out, it will be very difficult to do meaningful data analysis and improvement.

Finally, a Class A PM program incorporates the features of the first two levels, and takes them further by collecting data within the maintenance tasks in the PM program to improve the PMs themselves and the equipment being worked on. It is at this point that savings can be maximized through preventative maintenance and predictive maintenance (an advanced form of condition-based maintenance(CBM)) can be introduced as part of the overall work plan.

- **Autonomous (AM)**

<u>Why it is important:</u>

Autonomous Maintenance is a TPM term for operator or basic technician maintenance, which is necessary for the daily operation of the machine or process. Example: add oil to your car or clean circuit board tray after each shift. Usually, it is performed while the machine is running or requires less than 15 minutes of downtime and includes tasks which require only operating supplies (oil, grease, etc) to complete. Inspections, condition-based monitoring, taking system measurements, and cleaning can all be part of an AM program, which should be performed by the operating personnel.

Today, Autonomous Maintenance is one of the most overlooked parts of any maintenance program, by both the maintenance and operations managers. AM teaches discipline and team work to operating personnel as they have to complete the AM tasks in a regular manner in order to help the maintenance department keep their equipment operating properly.

Although, AM tasks are not normally finitely scheduled to the day and hour, a good AM program does collect readings, completion, and emergent work from each task. The readings and completion are very useful for CBM and improvement programs implemented by the maintenance manager. The emergent work can help tip off the maintenance manager to smaller problems before they become bigger ones and cause extended equipment downtime.

Class A Autonomous Maintenance programs incorporate all of these features and feed the other aspects of the total maintenance program. Their effect can be felt in every facet of maintenance from scheduling to improvement programs to long-term planning. If executed correctly, a good AM program can go a long way towards improving the maintenance bottom line.

Reactive and condition-based maintenance (RM & CBM)

<u>Why it is important:</u>

A reactive maintenance program is the catch-all for all other required maintenance work. It could be the result of an emergency, an improvement, safety issue, product upgrade, capital project or the result of other maintenance that monitors the performance of equipment (CBM). Basically, it is items not regularly planned but which must be done to keep business vital. It is important to document them not only to capture the work for future completion, but also additionally to review them for trends and future improvements.

Today, in most maintenance departments, RM makes up anywhere from 70-95% of all maintenance work performed. This is not class A. The goal of every maintenance program is to change that metric to make it 70-95% preventative or autonomous.

The way to achieve such a change is through having good PM and AM programs and using them in conjunction with the data collected from the RM tasks to make maintenance more predictive and pro-active in nature, rather than reactive. It may take a few years to get to a 95% non-reactive maintenance environment, but it can be achieved with consistent data analysis and the implementation of good improvement programs. It takes a complete team effort to reach such a goal, including operating and supply personnel, but at that point a reactive maintenance program is Class A and the maintenance technicians more closely resemble the Maytag repairman.

- **Backlogs**

<u>Why it is important:</u>

It is always important to have a complete list of maintenance tasks. A backlog usually holds the overdue and/or unscheduled maintenance that the planner is holding for future use. However, this practice is not Class A. In a Class A maintenance program, all maintenance is planned and scheduled for a specific day and time. If the work is missed or incomplete, a new future date is determined and the order is rescheduled. This keeps the work off the backlog and on the lead technician's planning schedule. Additionally, the maintenance planner can make sure the capacity limits are not exceeded or they can adjust the schedule to get below them as well.

The bottom line is to get maintenance planners out of the habit of being able to save work for later or choose to "get to it when we can get to it." If they are required to schedule and plan completion to a specific day and time they will be more inclined to meet it. If they consistently reschedule the work then maybe that indicates how necessary it really was. In addition, planners should start to be evaluated based on schedule achievement. When a maintenance department has these kinds of guidelines in place, the need for a backlog will disappear and it will become a Class A maintenance program.

Example Weekly Maintenance Schedule

	2/5 I	2/5 II	2/5 III	2/6 I	2/6 II	2/6 III	2/7I	2/7 II	2/7 III	2/8 I	2/8 II	2/8 III	2/9 I	2/9 II	2/9 III
PM and AM Items	A-D	a 1700-1900	F-I	J-L	N-P	c,d,e,f,g,h 0200-0600	R,S	T-V	Z-AC	AD-AF	k,l,m 1530-1700	AH-AJ	o,p,q,s 0700-1000	AM-AP	AS-AV
Reactive Work		E	b,c 0000-0200	M	Q	i,j 0500-0600		W	X,Y	AG	n 1700-1800			AK-AL	AQ	AR
Emergencies															
Master Production Schedule - Downtime Availability	None	1700-1900	0000 – 0200	None	None	0200 - 0600	None	None	None	None	1530-1800	None	0700-1000	None	None

I = 0700 - 1500

II = 1500 - 2300

III = 2300 - 0700

Capital letters are work orders to be completed while machines are running

Small letters are work orders to be completed during downtime

Reasons for downtime: production changeovers, outages, planned non-production time

Maintenance Planning and Execution

Purpose

The primary function of every maintenance department is to identify, plan, execute, document, and evaluate maintenance work. That over-simplifies what is probably the most complex and cross-functional department in a manufacturing plant, the maintenance department. Yet, next to maybe the training department, it is probably the most under-appreciated and -utilized as well. However, as already mentioned, in today's environment, maintenance is the last place where big money can be saved in manufacturing. While production and purchasing are squeezing every last penny out of their processes, there are nickels and dimes to be had in the maintenance process. However, in order to achieve such savings, it is essential to enable a detailed maintenance planning process and integrate it on an even playing field into the other processes within the plant.

The planning and performance of each aspect of the maintenance business, can basically be broken down into five Key Best Practice Areas. They are:

Planning, scheduling, and capacity utilization	Maintenance work can come from many sources and includes all PMs, reactive and emergency items. Maintenance planning and scheduling provides maintenance planners the data to know • who and what is needed • when and where • for how long • how many and allows planners to optimize the utilization of every resource
Priority systems	A method of determining level of precedence among work requirements. It can assist with order planning, scheduling, and allocation of resources for task completion.
Performing the work	Execution of the maintenance task including completing the follow-up documentation.
Reporting	Reviewing the records in the maintenance database for specific details to better understand the business.
Budgeting	The estimate of the total costs for a maintenance department or work center. It includes the number of personnel required and all of their associated expenses.

Most importantly, it is in the details of each Key Best Practice Area where money can be saved in your maintenance department. Implementing the learnings you get from this book will produce those savings and raise the overall level of the maintenance organization . At that point, Class A certification can be realized and the return on your maintenance investments start to return significantly.

Key Best Practice areas:

Planning, scheduling, and capacity utilization

Why it is important:

Maintenance planning, scheduling and capacity utilization is a very important part of any Class A maintenance program. It sets the framework for the operation of the entire department and how it relates to the rest of the plant.

Every morning when a maintenance planner comes in, most of them look at who's due in today, what jobs are due, and what parts are here, and make up their work plan. This is not maintenance planning, scheduling and capacity utilization. It is reacting to the events of the day and dispatching resources accordingly. This is exactly the paradigm which a Class A maintenance program avoids.

The best maintenance programs plan 80-90% of their maintenance work 30 days in advance and include a firm schedule of resources no less than two weeks in advance (longer if long lead items are required).

Planning, in this environment, looks at maintenance in an 18-month view. It looks at factors such as maintenance supply and demand and business goals every month. From there, an 18-month maintenance plan is developed which integrated into the production schedule and inventory plan.

Maintenance Continuous Planning Process (MCPP)

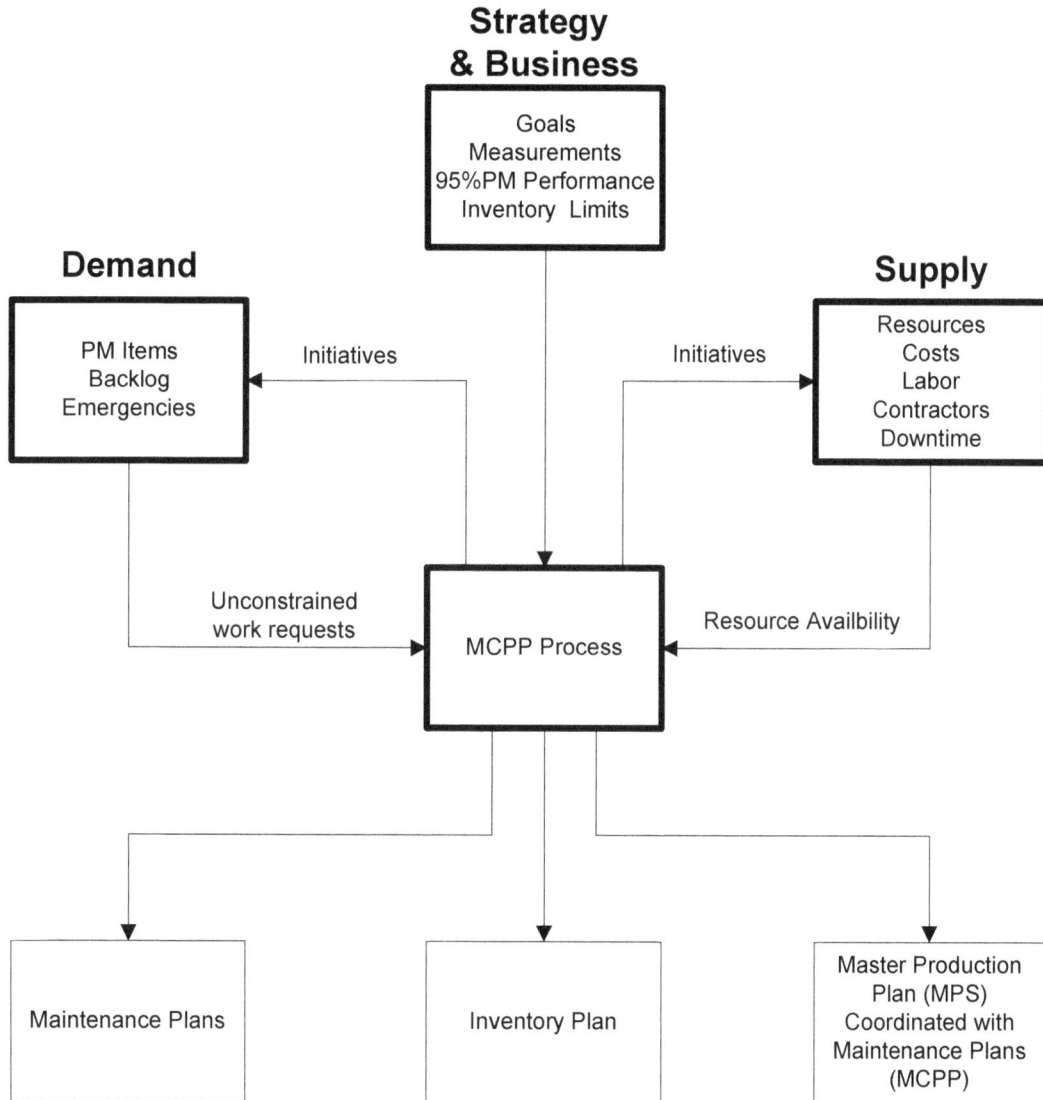

Strategy & Business

Goals
Measurements
95%PM Performance
Inventory Limits

Demand

PM Items
Backlog
Emergencies

Initiatives

Supply

Resources
Costs
Labor
Contractors
Downtime

Initiatives

Unconstrained
work requests

MCPP Process

Resource Availbility

Maintenance Plans

Inventory Plan

Master Production
Plan (MPS)
Coordinated with
Maintenance Plans
(MCPP)

That 18-month maintenance plan turns into the basis for the maintenance schedule 90 days prior to being executed (or longer for items with lead times greater than 90 days). The schedule should include all PM, AM and reactive items and available downtime blocks from the production schedule.

Example Weekly Maintenance

Schedule

(These start to be created 90 days in

advance)

	2/5 I	2/5 II	2/5 III	2/6 I	2/6 II	2/6 III	2/7 I	2/7 II	2/7 III	2/8 I	2/8 II	2/8 III	2/9 I	2/9 II	2/9 III
PM and AM Items	A-D	a 1700-1900	F-I	J-L	N-P	c,d,e,f,g,h 0200-0600	R,S	T-V	Z-AC	AD-AF	k,l,m 1530-1700	AH-AJ	o,p,q,s 0700-1000	AM-AP	AS-AV
Reactive Work		E	b,c 0000-0200	M	Q	i,j 0500-0600		W	X,Y	AG	n 1700-1800		AK-AL	AQ	AR
Emergencies															
Master Production Schedule - Down time Availability	None	1700-1900	0000-0200	None	None	0200-0600	None	None	None	None	1530-1800	None	0700-1000	None	None

I = 0700 - 1500

II = 1500 - 2300

III = 2300 - 0700

Capital letters are work orders to be completed while machines are running

Small letters are work orders to be completed during downtime

Reasons for downtime: production changeovers, outages, planned non-production time

As the maintenance execution gets closer, the schedule and resource allocation can be adjusted and refined to ensure completion on time and on schedule. However, 30 days before the maintenance event is executed, the order should be firmed up and finitely scheduled. Once inside 30 days, (in the firm zone) any changes to the schedule of an event must be at the concurrence of the production <u>and</u> maintenance departments.

It is at that point, resources begin to be issued and delivered to the work location and staged for execution. Three days before the scheduled start date, all resources are staged and available for the maintenance event at or near the work location. Thus, anytime unplanned downtime occurs in those 3 days, the maintenance event can be completed. While the cause of the downtime is worked, the other maintenance event can be forward-scheduled and executed at the same time as the event causing downtime. This maximizes the unplanned downtime and leads to less downtime scheduled later or the completion of more work in that downtime block. Either way, it's a win-win for maintenance and production.

Maintenance Planning and Scheduling Timeline

(c) 1998,
Steve Hampson

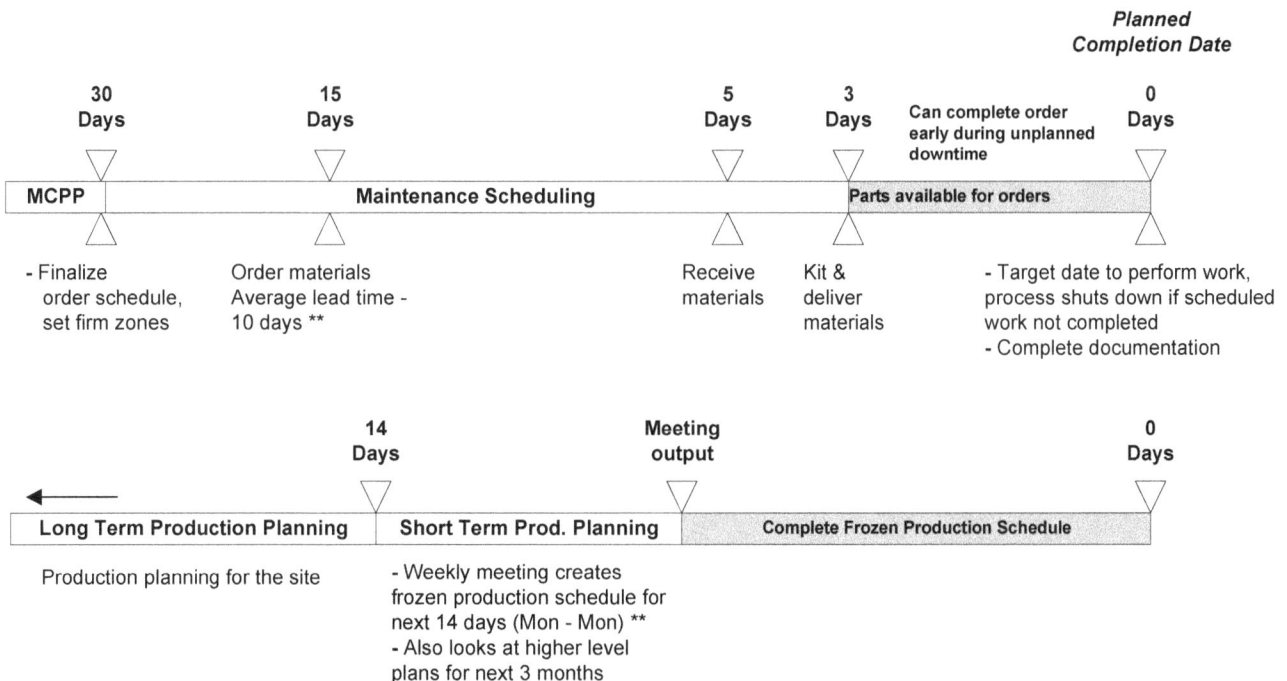

Planned Completion Date

| 30 Days | 15 Days | 5 Days | 3 Days | Can complete order early during unplanned downtime | 0 Days |

| MCPP | Maintenance Scheduling | | Parts available for orders |

- Finalize order schedule, set firm zones | Order materials Average lead time - 10 days ** | Receive materials | Kit & deliver materials | - Target date to perform work, process shuts down if scheduled work not completed - Complete documentation

| 14 Days | Meeting output | 0 Days |

| Long Term Production Planning | Short Term Prod. Planning | Complete Frozen Production Schedule |

Production planning for the site | - Weekly meeting creates frozen production schedule for next 14 days (Mon - Mon) ** - Also looks at higher level plans for next 3 months

** Will vary at each company

The maintenance planner plays a key role in the execution of such a forward-leaning maintenance program. First, they must have the maintenance planning and scheduling and parameters in place. Next, they must have integrated resource utilization into such a plan. Resources are defined as:

- Labor
    Skills
    Effort hours
- Materials

BOMs – for technical objects provide standardized parts lists, which may make it easier for standard material allocations for orders
Pre-planned parts directly link to material planning for storeroom requirements

- Contractors
    Contractor planning through SAP
- Special Tools
    Special "needs" planning – Ex: fork truck, test equipment
- Costs
    On-demand budgeting available in orders
    Cost planning for plans, work centers, and cost centers

With the planning and scheduling in place, the maintenance planner can review their resource utilization and see what items can be forward scheduled. The ultimate goal of this Key Best Practice Area is to make the best possible use of all the available resources and eliminate a backlog of work – thus increasing efficiencies and maintenance performance, reducing costs, and enabling a detailed continuous improvement program based on a defined workplan. Even if the planning and scheduling parameters are not as long as those described here, any maintenance department with processes in place that thinks along these lines is definitely on the road to Class A. For more information on the details of such a program, see Appendix C, Maintenance Continuous Planning Program (MCPP).

- **Priority systems**

Why it is important:

A <u>very</u> helpful tool for a maintenance planner in maintenance planning, scheduling, and capacity utilization is a maintenance prioritization system. An objective prioritization system allows maintenance planners to make resource and planning decisions based on data and pre-established plant priorities instead of the latest input by superiors. If your plant's priority system looks like your organization chart, it is not Class A.

Actually the best priority systems are not only used objectively, but are two-pronged. The first prong is a plant-wide equipment/location priority system. This system looks at overall plant processes, safety, process bottlenecks, downstream effects, business goals, costs, etc and assigns a value to the equipment/location which is reviewed and updated each quarter. Usually the rankings are assigned at the line/process/sub-process level and rolled down to subordinate equipment (much more detail is a data management problem).

Example Equipment/Location Ranking Chart

Item	Factors Evaluated	Rank 1	Rank 2	Rank 3	Rank 4
Points		**3**	**2**	**1**	**0**
Safety	Malfunction's effect on the outside environment?	Failure to complete work violates health and/or safety operating standards	X	X	None
Production	What is the reliability required to meet the production needs?	90% reliability needed	80% reliability needed	65% reliability needed	Less than 50% reliability needed
	Are there other alternatives in case of failure?	No alternatives available	Production can be delayed	Production covered by stock or other	Alternate equipment available
	How does this equipment/ location affect other processes?	Affects the entire plant	Other processes are unable to meet their production requirements	Minimal effect on other processes	No effect

Facilities

Quality	How do the results of this equipment/ location affect finished product quality?	Product completed undeliverable	Defective finished products greater than 5%	Defective finished products less than 5%	No effect
	What percentage of scrap produced is caused by the equipment/ location?	10% or greater	5 - 10%	2 - 5%	0 - 2%
Reliability	What percentage of maintenance downtime is caused by this equipment/ location?	10% or greater	5 - 10%	2 - 5%	0 - 2%
Maintenance Issues	What is the cost effectiveness of delaying maintenance at this equipment/ location?	Delay will incur costs greater than 10 times cost of the work	Delay will incur costs 5 to 10 times cost of the work	Delay will incur costs less than 5 times cost of the work	No effect
	What percentage of average actual monthly maintenance costs are against this functional location?	10% or greater	5 - 10%	2 - 5%	0 - 2%

**Equipment/
Location Ranking**
   A = 27 - 25
   B = 24 - 22
   C = 21 - 19
   D = 18 - 16

E = 15 - 13

F = 12 - 10

G = 9 - 7

H = 6 - 4

I = 3 - 0

For each equipment /location, answer each question above.

Add the point totals for each answer to get the total point value for the equipment/location.

Compare that number against the priority table to determine equipment/location priority.

Letter A is highest priority

This process is to be conducted quarterly by plant.

The second maintenance prioritization program is more specific to the maintenance event itself. It asks, "How important is this event to the operation and functionality of the problem equipment?" and gives input to the scheduler as to how soon the event should be executed.

Example Event Priority System

E - Emergency

N - Next planned downtime

R - Routine

O – Next outage

Note: Preventative maintenance orders in Class A maintenance programs do not have an assigned priority. You should have a PM program you are committed to and perform as planned. Not only will it keep up the machine's productivity but if PMs are not performed regularly, consistent data can not be generated well enough to know what items are worth doing and which should be deleted.

By using these two objective maintenance prioritization programs, the planner has a truly plant-wide perspective of the reactive maintenance problems and can balance their planning, schedule, and capacity utilization accordingly. The truly objective resource planning based on data resulting from a good prioritization program is a critical factor in any Class A maintenance program and is a significant contributor to any savings realized in the maintenance planning and execution key area.

- **Performing the work**

Why it is important:

Performing maintenance work is the task that makes maintenance people essential to any factory. They keep the line/process/equipment in the best possible operating condition to maximize production capacity. However, that job not only includes the hands-on maintenance, but also the documentation that is required as well.

Completing a work task in the correct manner is the key part of any maintenance person's job. In addition, they must also provide complete documentation for the maintenance program to continue smoothly and enable the continuous improvement program.

At a minimum, a Class A maintenance execution program starts with the technician gathering the required materials and documentation for the maintenance task and verifies their correctness. If there are any shortfalls, the technician resolves them prior to commencing work.

Once the maintenance is complete, the technician must complete the follow-up documentation. This work includes parts and labor usage, recommendations for improvements to the item or maintenance event, updating the maintenance database records, and readying the original work order for close and/or creating a new order for emergent work.

Finally, the technician tags all remaining materials for return to storeroom and identifies which are repairable. The storeroom personnel pick up the materials from the maintenance site and transport them to the storeroom.

Example
Maintenance Execution
Process

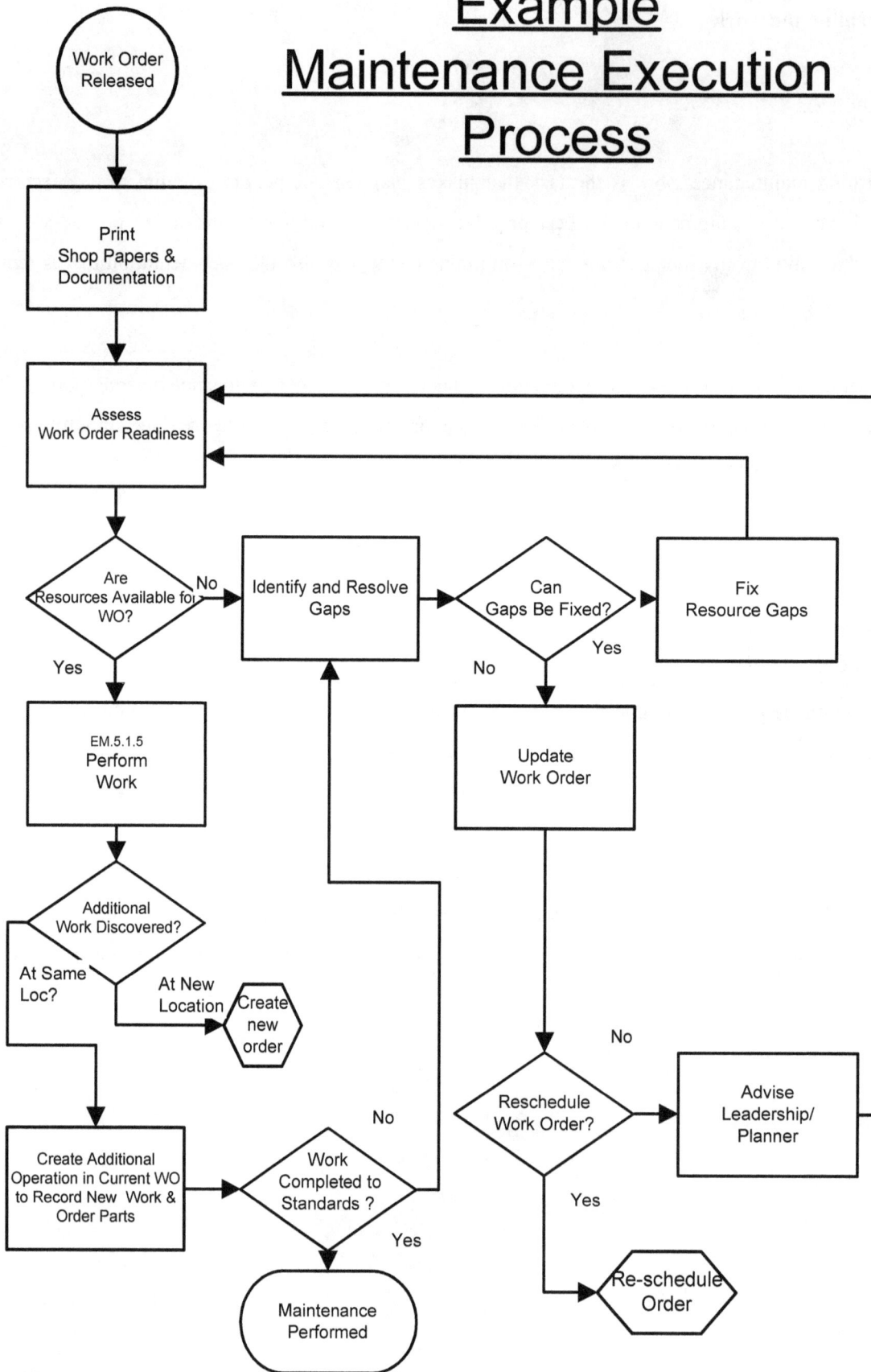

Work Order Released

Print Shop Papers & Documentation

Assess Work Order Readiness

Are Resources Available for WO?

No → **Identify and Resolve Gaps** → **Can Gaps Be Fixed?**

Yes → **Fix Resource Gaps**

No → **Update Work Order**

Yes (from Are Resources Available) → **EM.5.1.5 Perform Work**

Additional Work Discovered?

At Same Loc?

At New Location → **Create new order**

Create Additional Operation in Current WO to Record New Work & Order Parts

Work Completed to Standards?

No

Yes → **Maintenance Performed**

Reschedule Work Order?

No → **Advise Leadership/ Planner**

Yes → **Re-schedule Order**

Once the technician completes the work, the work center leader reviews the documentation and makes comments/recommendations as necessary and closes the work order.

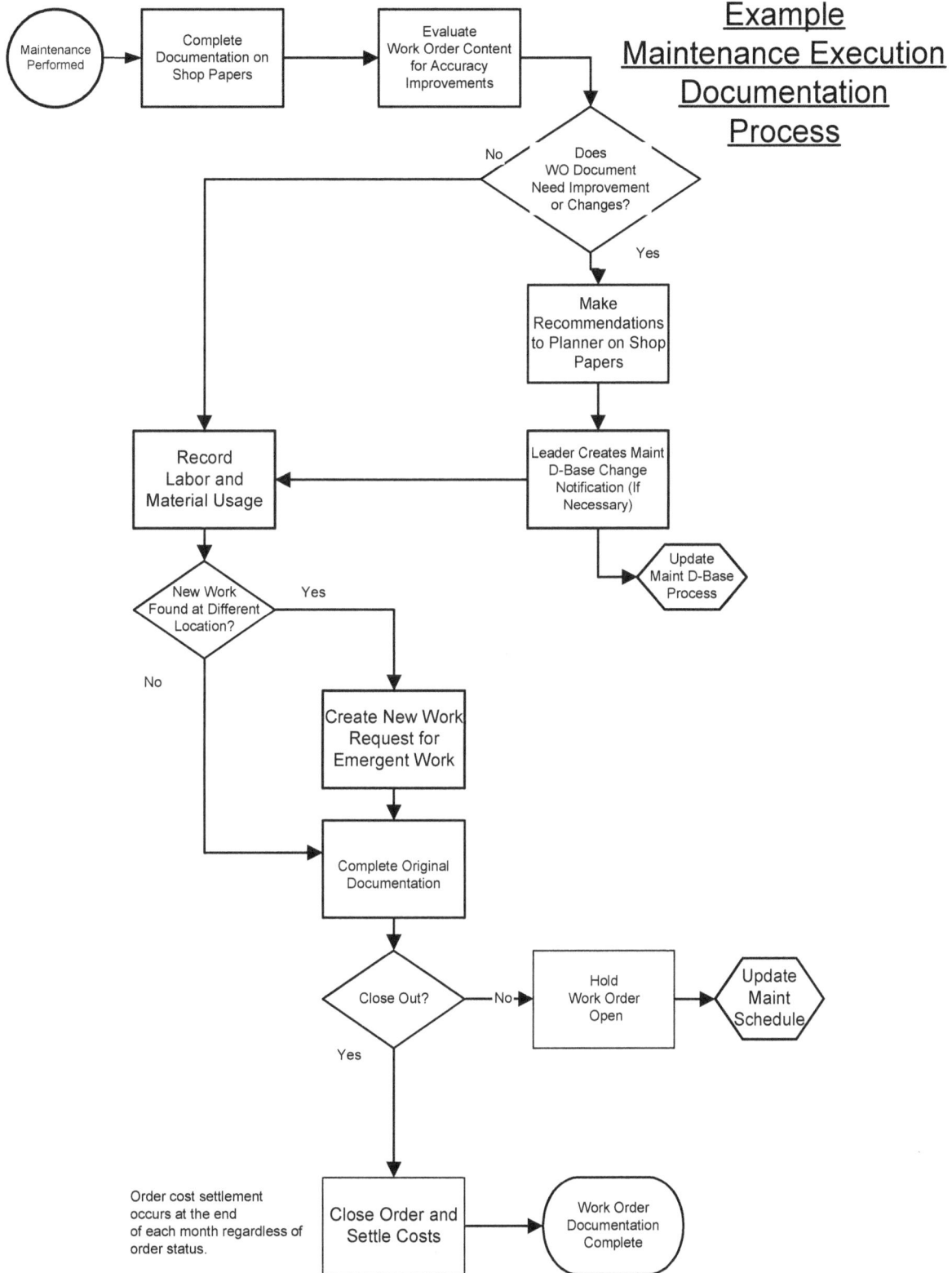

Example Maintenance Execution Documentation Process

```
[Maintenance Performed] → [Complete Documentation on Shop Papers] → [Evaluate Work Order Content for Accuracy Improvements]
                                                                              ↓
                                                            <Does WO Document Need Improvement or Changes?>
                                         No ←                                           → Yes
                                         ↓                                               ↓
                                                                           [Make Recommendations to Planner on Shop Papers]
                                                                                         ↓
              [Record Labor and Material Usage] ← [Leader Creates Maint D-Base Change Notification (If Necessary)]
                            ↓                                                            ↓
                  <New Work Found at Different Location?> — Yes               ⬡ Update Maint D-Base Process
                            ↓ No                            ↓
                                              [Create New Work Request for Emergent Work]
                                                            ↓
                            → [Complete Original Documentation]
                                                            ↓
                                                    <Close Out?> — No → [Hold Work Order Open] → ⬡ Update Maint Schedule
                                                            ↓ Yes
   Order cost settlement
   occurs at the end
   of each month regardless of     [Close Order and Settle Costs] → (Work Order Documentation Complete)
   order status.
```

Performing the maintenance work should be considered more than just turning the wrenches to solve problems. It's the end of a long maintenance process that has several steps leading to its execution, as well as enabling several downstream improvement processes. Effective and efficient maintenance execution is what maintenance departments are created for, but the Class A maintenance departments do all the other aspects of maintenance just as well. This enables the development of savings and improvement programs, which in turn leads to less "firefighting" and more planning: the new maintenance paradigm in Class A maintenance.

- **Reporting**

Why it is important:

Maintenance reporting allows managers the opportunity to review the information in the database to understand the status of the operation, to look for trends and recommend possible improvements. Class A maintenance programs process the collection of a lot of data for later analysis. It is the reporting measures sections that audit the success of such programs. Some maintenance reports include: location and equipment history, including PM and production performance, labor and material usage and costs, and planned vs. actual data. Also, comparisons across similar locations and equipments in the same or different business areas are often available.

Ultimately there are three reasons for reporting. They are:

- Understanding current status
- Performance and cost analysis
- Continuous Improvement

A well-structured reporting database and clear reporting and evaluation goals are the tools to reaching the savings and improvement goals. It is at this point that data is analyzed and turned into improvement activities, thus managing based on data and working towards Class A certification.

- **Budgeting**

Why it is important:

Budgeting and budget performance are primary evaluation criteria for most plant leadership. Thus, every supervisor and planner is required to provide at least annual cost estimates for a maintenance budget. This provides for cost tracking and analysis as the year progresses as well as history for future comparison.

In a Class A maintenance program, there exists a large amount of data to draw from for each year's budget (historical data, 18 month maintenance plan, capacity utilization, etc.) It is important that this data is collected and presented properly and completely in order to present the most accurate picture to plant leadership.

The process begins with determining estimated costs for each work center. The costs include the number of personnel required and their expenses. Also, a factor for unplanned downtime is calculated here from past performance of this work center, based on previous planned vs. actual usage – how much of their labor will be spent against planned and unplanned downtime. These values will be used to help determine the labor rate for the work center.

A. Estimate the total costs for the following items for the personnel in your work center:

- Travel
- Training
- Wages
- Benefits
- Vacations
- Consumables
- Meetings
- Overtime

B. Based on previous performance, estimate a percentage of production time lost due to unplanned downtime.

The next step is to determine total maintenance labor hours allocated to planned maintenance for the next fiscal year for your work center and review the next year's maintenance plan for PM, AM, and reactive maintenance activities. The result should be total planned maintenance hours for the upcoming fiscal year.

The third step is to submit the total planned hours + total unplanned hours, and the personnel requirements, to the accounting department for determination of the annual labor rate.

Once that rate is determined, the total maintenance costs can be determined for the next fiscal year. To get the expected labor costs, multiply the labor rate by the expected hours. To get the resource costs, review the maintenance plan and schedules (MCPP) and calculate the totals.

Finally, collect all expected costs in a clear and concise manner and submit them for the next fiscal year. From the budget and the MCPP, maintenance managers can justify needs with data and show what cuts/increases mean in costs, reliability, downstream problems, etc.

Material Planning

Purpose

Material planning through a totally integrated storeroom and purchasing system provides the most streamlined process to support the tasks of the maintenance department. Thus, it is critical that these two departments work together to ensure the success of one another.

Examples of areas where they are closely linked include:

As more maintenance is planned, inventory levels at sites can be reduced and moved further back in the supply chain, resulting in lower carrying costs to both the site and the supplier.

A common, standardized parts numbering system provides maintenance personnel one resource for parts procurement, thus not driving up inventories while ordering the wrong parts or something that may already be available but under a different number.

Thus, the long-term success of these two departments depends on how well they work together. A company can usually achieve significant savings by getting a good handle on their material needs through maintenance planning and removing no-longer-needed parts from their inventory.

However, in order to maximize the efficiencies of the maintenance and material departments, these five Key Best Practice Areas must be considered:

Output of planning systems and ability to meet needs	Integrating maintenance work planning systems with material planning systems to share data and determine/meet material needs
Supplier involvement	The level of involvement between a plant and its suppliers in determining plant inventory.
Stock usage, safety stock, leveraged purchasing	Understanding the stock requirements from planned and unplanned maintenance tasks and developing a formula for determining safety stock levels. That formula can be rolled into the overall material plan to enable grouped purchasing for the site/company.
Parts inventory process	Identifying which parts and how many of each is on hand and in what location at a plant.
Parts delivery process (to work area)	Bringing the parts required for a maintenance task from the storeroom to the maintenance area.

At a minimum, these areas identify the five most integral links between maintenance and the storeroom. The goal of every Class A maintenance program is to accurately plan, purchase, and deliver the material needs of the maintenance department to the correct areas in a timely manner. By involving the storeroom in the overall maintenance plan, significant near term savings improvements can be achieved.

Key Best Practice areas:

- **Output of planning systems and ability to meet needs**

<u>Why it is important:</u>

The process to plan material needs for the storeroom entails planning to meet the demand for materials from the maintenance operation and receiving them in time for maintenance execution. The MRP (Material Requirements Planning) process can assess the material requirements of the maintenance organization and determine the best resource fulfillment strategy (e.g. make, buy, pull from stock). The computer can then automatically plan the fulfillment of the requirement based on item lead time and due date parameters (e.g. received due date + 5 days).

Thus to best enable a Class A material planning process, material planning data should be shared across maintenance and material planning systems. Significant cost savings would be achieved through long-range planning and leveraged purchasing of known requirements across multiple lines/processes or plants. In addition, inventories would be lower with JIT purchasing. Finally, total parts costs would decrease because parts purchasing would be planned and not regularly expedited, driving up delivery costs. All of these factors contribute to a better bottom line for the maintenance and material departments.

- **Supplier involvement**

<u>Why it is important:</u>

In a Class A material planning environment, suppliers work with companies to streamline the supply pipe for both parties. They keep their customers' inventories down by providing them with parts on a just-in-time basis. This helps customers keep down inventory storage costs which helps suppliers meet their customers' needs on a more planned, regular basis. Suppliers do this by working with their customer to get data from the customer's MRP and inventory process, which is fed by the maintenance planning process.

Supply Pipe
(Notice no elbows or Valves)

| MCPP | MRP | Storeroom Inventory Levels | Supplier Inventory Levels | Supplier Production Plans |

1/1/2003   7/2/2003

It is the kind of information sharing which can be very beneficial to both parties. Ultimately the goal is for suppliers and customers to work together on resource requirements far enough in advance to help manage inventory levels and production requirements. Thus, the "Supply Pipe" is much more direct and efficient and savings can be considerable for both parties.

- **Stock usage, safety stock, leveraged purchasing**

Why it is important:

In a Class A Material Management program, understanding the parts inventory can lead to significant savings in two ways. One, parts can quickly be identified as not often used and/or out of date from work order history or plant configuration data. These parts can then be used and not replaced, sold off, or scrapped and removed from inventory, thus cutting inventory costs.

Secondly, shelf-life data can give storeroom personnel a better idea of material turn over and can stock the shelves at the correct levels and locations. This also can lead to lower inventories, leveraged purchasing, and faster order fulfillment. In each case, it can lead to increased savings for a plant.

The goal should be to not only have the right materials but to have the right amounts and distribute them as efficiently as possible to the maintenance event.

- **Parts inventory process**

Why it is important:

Inventory Record Accuracy (IRA) is a key part of every material planning effort. If an accurate picture of what materials are on hand is not available, the results can be not nearly as efficient and could even be very dubious.

IRA is imperative to the cost effective operation of the maintenance and material business. A high IRA ensures that the correct parts are in the correct locations and can be reserved correctly by maintenance planners. Inaccuracies here drive up inventories and costs. Therefore, it is very critical to keep IRA at the highest possible levels (ideally > 98%)

IRA is defined as the percentage of inventory record items which agree with the physical stock on hand for quantity, within a specified tolerance, location, and status. A correct IRA requires that all criteria are met.

IRA Calculation:

$$\text{Inventory Record Accuracy \%} = \frac{\text{Number of Correct Items}}{\text{Total Number of Items Checked}}$$

There are several reasons why an accurate inventory is useful. First, in order to know what is available at a location, where it is, and how many are available. Accurate inventory makes the maintenance and material process more efficient.

Secondly, it allows the material planning personnel to be able to monitor costs and turnover and adjust their plans accordingly. This provides for the most accurate and cost effective planning and purchasing process.

Thirdly, the accounting department tracks inventory and its value as it flows to the bottom line. This provides the leadership and shareholders with an accurate picture of how the company is operating.

Thus, every Class A maintenance department must have a storeroom which supports it with an IRA of 98% or better. Without it, not only will there be many questions regarding what a storeroom has and where it is, but why does my inventory cost so much and what am I adding to it by purchasing things I later find I already have? This is the tip of the iceberg but, needless to say, significant, very visible dollars can be saved by meeting Class A standards in this Key Business Area.

- **Parts delivery process (to work area)**

Why it is important:

In a Class A material planning program, all parts requests are filled by the storeroom personnel. They have the tools at their disposal to take orders, track them, and receive them into a storage location. In addition, they are responsible for bringing the parts to the maintenance area when the task is nearly ready to be performed.

This makes both the storeroom and maintenance personnel more efficient. Maintenance personnel no longer have to make trips to storerooms throughout the plant to retrieve parts. The storeroom personnel will not be bothered by interruptions from the maintenance people. They can plan materials to arrive just in time and, instead of putting them on the shelves, they can store them in temporary storage locations near the work stations for the maintenance personnel to use as soon as they are ready to start the work, thus saving stocking and re-issue time.

In addition, when materials come in, they are immediately assigned to an order. This makes storeroom accounting easier and prevents the piling up of parts for no reason

Because of increased efficiencies, storeroom personnel have more time for parts delivery in a Class A maintenance program. Usually their delivery is in bulk once or twice a day and/or shift. Sometimes it's not by personnel but machines. Regardless, a more efficient process is carried out by both maintenance and storeroom personnel to the benefit of both.

In a Class A maintenance department, maintenance personnel concentrate on the planning and execution of maintenance events. With a good integrated material planning process for maintenance in place, storeroom personnel can be responsible for materials once they are requested up to the time of maintenance execution.

Measures

Purpose

As discussed previously, Class A maintenance programs collect a great deal of data. Every plant has a set of well-defined, well-known success measures for their maintenance business. This helps people identify their performance and that of their equipment and clearly indicate positive and negative trends in both. From these numbers, areas can be identified for improvement. A continuous improvement program should be in place and provide a consistent and recurring effort towards meeting measured business goals.

In addition, a good data analysis program should be in place to filter through all maintenance database information, identifying trends, and making improvements as well. These types of programs can be more technical in design and usually lead to developments like changes in equipment, operating methods, and maintenance processes.

The two key Best Practice Areas listed below must be incorporated into every best-in-class maintenance department. They are:

Success Measures	Statistics which can gauge the overall performance of a line/process or business
Data analysis & continuous improvement	Reviewing the records in the maintenance database for specific details as outlined in the reporting document to better understand the business and make improvements

A maintenance department that has incorporated such a continuous improvement process in a routine and robust manner is clearly well down the road toward Class A certification and is achieving <u>real</u> savings and improvements on a very regular basis.

Key Best Practice areas:

- **Success Measures**

<u>Why it is important:</u>

Success measures look at business goals set forth by leadership and tracks performance against them. A good set of success criteria can be very useful in evaluating the performance of a line/process or business. Supervisors can use the data to identify trends and recommend improvements. In addition, personnel can be held to clearly defined standards, which can be easily determined.

This is key to the success of any Class A maintenance program: having business goals and standards and holding your people to them. It is very difficult, especially in large organizations, for companies to hold personnel to standards they don't measure, report, and evaluate. Thus, a good measurement program is critical to keep a maintenance department leaning forward towards problem solving and improvement efforts. This will ensure new savings opportunities are regularly developed as well as previous ones already implemented being adhered to.

Example measures include:

- Benchmarking and comparison for improvements
- Parts usage data
- Problem reports
- Breakdown data
- Cost analysis
- Chronic losses – small, frequent deviations from optimal operating conditions which gradually become accepted as normal. Usually, they require breakthrough or innovative improvements to restore the machine or component to optimal operating condition.
- Sporadic losses – sudden, often larger deviations from optimal operating conditions. Usually, they have a single, obvious cause, which is correctable.

- **Data analysis & continuous improvement**

Why it is important:

Data analysis and continuous improvement looks at all the historical information in the maintenance database to find opportunities for improvement.

There are several ways this kind of program can be successful. One option is to look at the top 10 most frequent problems each year and perform root cause analysis on each one to find a solution and have it in place by the end of the year. Others look at the 10 most costly or 10 problems that impact productivity the most.

Regardless, the goal of every Class A data analysis and continuous improvement program is to look for process and/or design improvements which can better the maintenance business and deliver cost improvements. Any departments which have these processes in place and provide step-change improvements is certainly Class A

Example Data Analysis and Improvement Implementation

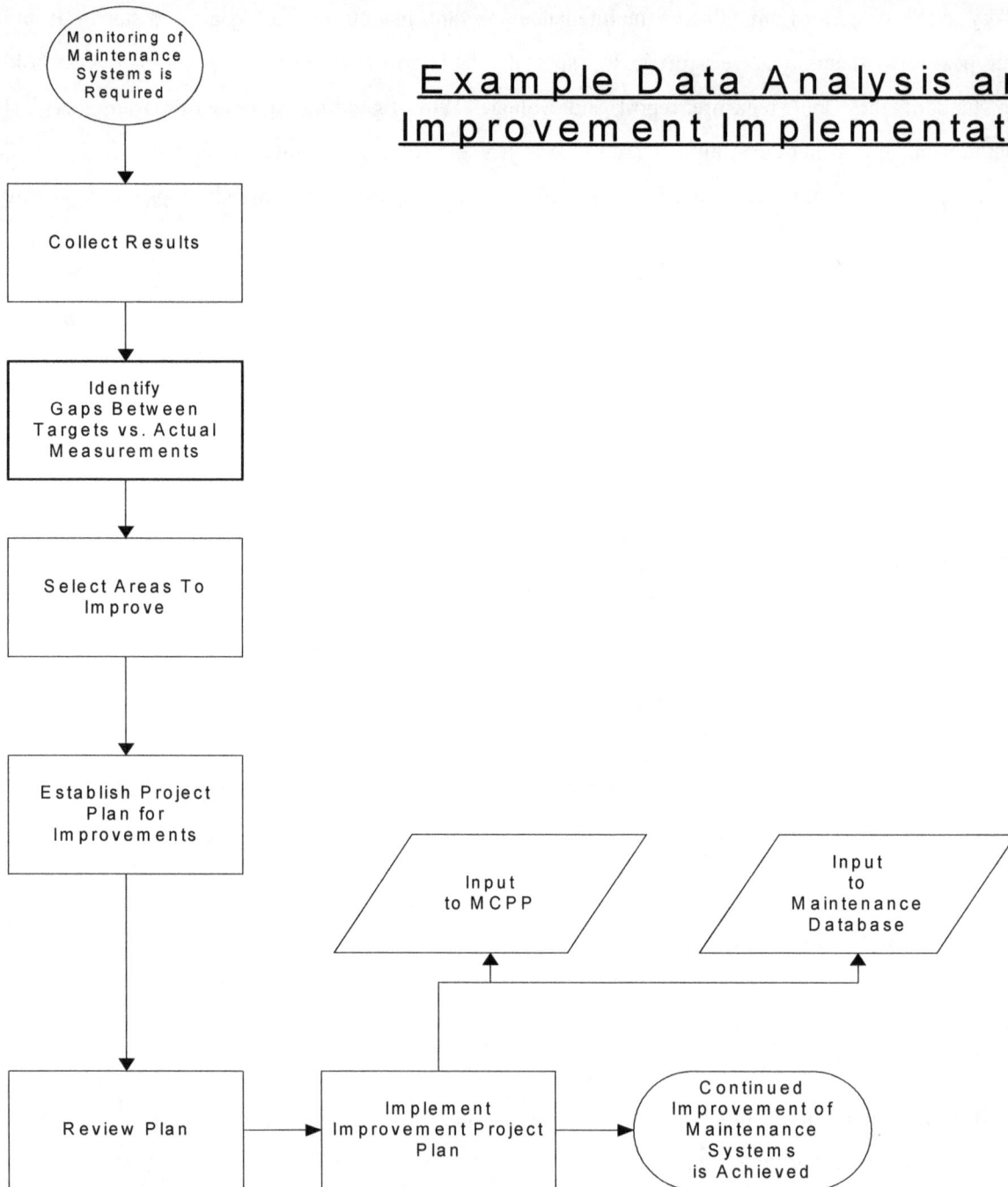

```
        ( Monitoring of
          Maintenance
          Systems is
          Required )
              |
              v
    +------------------+
    |  Collect Results |
    +------------------+
              |
              v
    +------------------+
    |     Identify     |
    |  Gaps Between    |
    | Targets vs. Actual|
    |  Measurements    |
    +------------------+
              |
              v
    +------------------+
    | Select Areas To  |
    |     Improve      |
    +------------------+
              |
              v
    +------------------+
    | Establish Project|
    |    Plan for      |
    |  Improvements    |
    +------------------+
              |
              v
    +------------------+        +------------------+
    |   Review Plan    | -----> |    Implement     |
    +------------------+        | Improvement Project
                                |       Plan       |
                                +------------------+
```

Input to MCPP

Input to Maintenance Database

Continued Improvement of Maintenance Systems is Achieved

Organizational Effectiveness

Purpose

Although it may be taken for granted, the organization structure of a maintenance department can go a long way towards determining its daily success or failure. The goal of every Class A maintenance department should be to structure each facet of the maintenance work environment in order to maximize its efficiency. Doing this correctly will enable many of the best practices identified previously and bring everything together to one common maintenance vision based on planning, execution and data analysis.

The three key factors of organizational effectiveness are:

Organizational structure	The representation of how personnel are organized within a plant
Specific maintenance philosophies	A methodology for operating the maintenance department
Computer systems	The computers or CMMS (Computerized Maintenance Management Systems) which help enable the maintenance business.

With these three items successfully in place, the foundation of any Class A maintenance program is sound and its potential is boundless.

Key Best Practice areas:

• **Organizational structure**

<u>Why it is important:</u>

Maintenance organizations are built on three foundations: people, business practices and information. How successful these organizations are depends solely on how well these elements work together. The organizational structure must be set up to streamline the maintenance planning and performance processes as well as ensure the results are shared across the department and with other key points in the company.

It is when the responsibility and goals of each employee is clearly laid out that they can function in the most efficient manner. In addition, with clear rules in place, systems can help employees meet goals while enforcing the rules in place. This is a win-win for technicians and management.

It is this kind of working environment that is Class A and can best enable the other Class A business practices discussed previously.

Sample Maintenance Organizational Chart

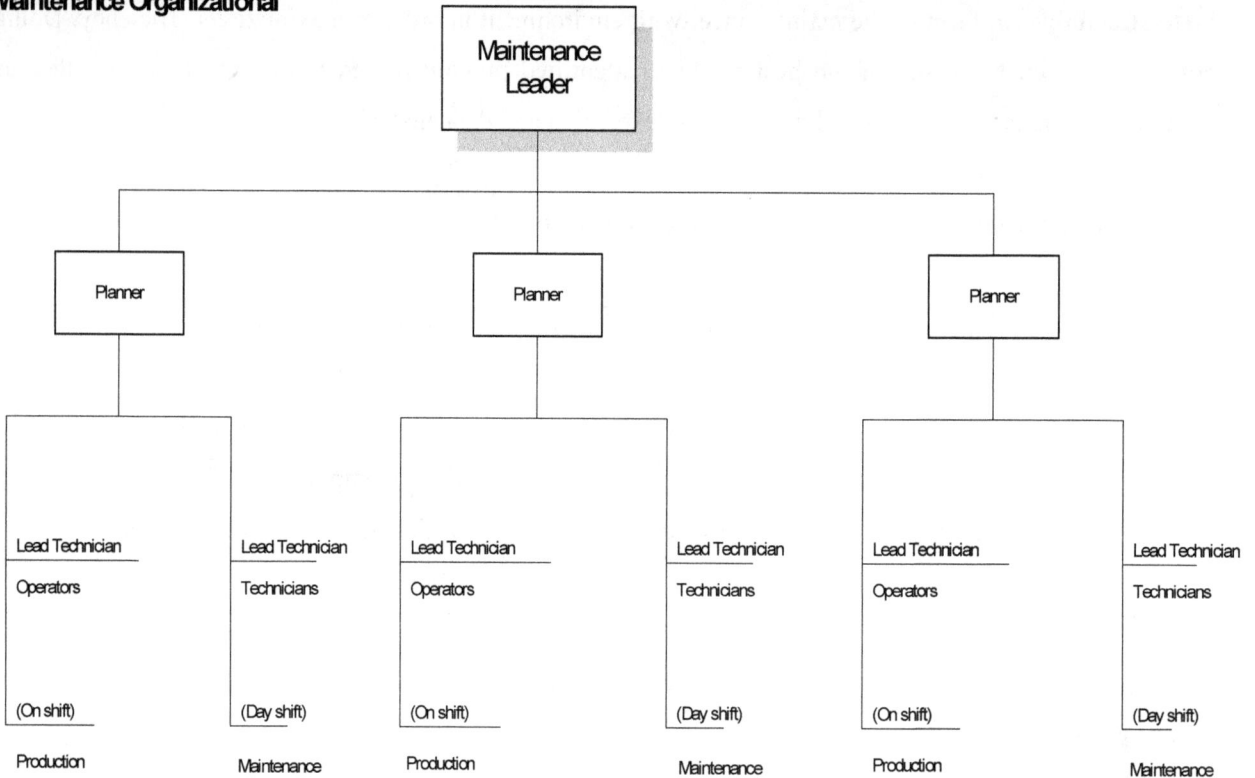

```
                              ┌──────────────┐
                              │  Maintenance │
                              │    Leader    │
                              └──────────────┘
                                     │
        ┌────────────────────────────┼────────────────────────────┐
        │                            │                            │
   ┌─────────┐                  ┌─────────┐                  ┌─────────┐
   │ Planner │                  │ Planner │                  │ Planner │
   └─────────┘                  └─────────┘                  └─────────┘
```

Lead Technician	Lead Technician	Lead Technician	Lead Technician	Lead Technician	Lead Technician
Operators	Technicians	Operators	Technicians	Operators	Technicians
(On shift)	(Day shift)	(On shift)	(Day shift)	(On shift)	(Day shift)
Production	Maintenance	Production	Maintenance	Production	Maintenance

- **Specific maintenance philosophies**

Why it is important:

There are several maintenance philosophies in use today. However, the most effective are those that integrate maintenance needs with all parts of the business. Maintenance deals directly with every part of the company, from sales to production, purchasing to finance. The maintenance philosophy that can integrate the most aspects of the company is the most effective.

Class A maintenance programs incorporate the principles of this philosophy with others such as TPM or TQ to provide the best possible structure and business goals for your maintenance department.

- **Computer systems**

<u>Why it is important:</u>

Computers are very effective in the managing and storing of data. With all the data collection and analysis requirements in Class A maintenance, it is essential to have a CMMS in place. There are several CMMS providers in the marketplace, but there are two key factors to consider when choosing one that will meet Class A standards.

The first is how well will the CMMS integrate with other aspects of your plant's business. The more closely production, finance, purchasing, inventory management, etc can be linked to maintenance, the better.

Secondly, how well will a CMMS enable AIT devices? With technology getting smaller and cheaper, Class A maintenance programs should consider hand held devices such as PDAs or text pagers to automate their maintenance business practices. AIT devices provide the opportunity for significant return on investment when it comes to time and data collection/reporting efficiencies and would go a long way towards solving data collection issues that may arise with the implementation of a CMMS or of Class A business practices.

The goal of every Class a maintenance program should be to implement an integrated CMMS with AIT devices. The opportunities for efficiency improvement and cost savings are numerous and pay for themselves in weeks instead of years.

Class A Maintenance Certification Audit

The next six sections contain the specific questions around certifying your maintenance program Class A. In order to not make the size of the book overwhelming, the answers for scoring are included after each question. Many of the questions have point values which can be totaled in section 10 "Scoring Information and Totals." Those that do not, are baseline questions which helps the auditor get a better feel for the maintenance department they are reviewing. In total, there are over 450 questions to help conduct a broad and deep review of the maintenance organizations business processes and better drive out areas for improvement.

Plant Data Structure

- **Plant equipment and/or location structure**

A record created for a piece of equipment within a plant

Plant structure:

1. Is the facility/factory/site numbered?

Yes = 1 1/3

2. If yes, how? To what level of detail? E.g. sequentially through the process flow, geographically, or otherwise intelligently numbered?

Describe:

The best method is through process flow and geography
E.g: Line 1, process 2, section 6, part 4
Line 7, process 4, section 1, part 3

Level of detail:
Line   + 2/3
Process   + 2/3
Section   + 2/3
Part   + 2/3

3. What is your company's definition of a piece of equipment?

No points

A specific piece of equipment where you want to track the repair and cost history of that particular item throughout its useful life, regardless of its location.

4. List all other productive and non-productive (support systems) items which are part of your plant's PM program.

E.g. cooling & heating systems, fire-extinguishing systems, electrical systems…

Computer support systems, building exterior and interior

No points

Long list…

5.   Are there items such as motor, pumps, and/or product sizing assemblies, which rotate in and out of the production process?

Yes / No   No points

6.   If yes, what are they?

No points

Long list…

7.   Do they rotate in and out of the same location or can they be installed at other locations in the same and/or different production processes?

No points

8.   At what levels of your plant machinery hierarchy is history kept? E.g. plant, line/process, specific equipment, etc.

Plant	1
Line/process	2
Specific Assembly	3
Component	4

9.   What Percentage of PM data is at each level?

Component > 75%	4
Component > 50% and Assembly > 25%	3
Component > 25% and Assembly >50 %	2
Assembly > 50 % and Line/Process > 25%	1.5

Assembly > 25% and Line/Process >50%   1

Line Process > 50% and Plant > 25%   .5

10. What kind of history is kept? E.g. Costs, PMs, breakdowns, parts usage, productivity

List them

No points

11. Where is it kept?

Integrated database (SAP)   4

Computerized Maintenance Management System (CMMS)   2.5

Card file, notebook, file cabinet 1

Continuous Improvement

12. What do you do with your historical data regularly?

List them

No points

Reports, data analysis, continuous improvement

13. How often?

Monthly or sooner   4

Quarterly   3

Semi-Annually   2

Annually   1

14. Is analysis done on this data?

Yes / No   No points

15. If so, what kinds?

List them

No points

Improvement feedback

16. Is the outcome of the analysis fed back to the process?

Yes / No   Yes = 1 1/3

17. Are improvements applied to process immediately?

Yes / No   Yes = 1 1/3

18. Are improvements to process shared immediately?

Yes / No   Yes = 1 1/3

- **Bills of Material (BOMs)**

A group of materials, which make up a specific object or are required for a task.

1. Do you have Bills of Material in your plant?

Yes / No   No points

2. What are they used for? E.g. Production, maintenance, purchasing, shipping, accounting…

Give an example of each use you mention.

List them

No points

Production for product
Maintenance for maintenance, to repair Equip
To ship item

3. How were they created? From what reference?

No points

4. What is in them and to what level of detail? E.g. Parts, documents, assemblies

List them

No points

5. How are the following issues covered:

Substitutions when BOM parts are not in stock

6. Are they permitted?

Yes / No   No = 4 (skip to 10), Yes = 0

7.   If so, in what cases?

Only 1 instance +1

8.   With whose authorization?
Authorization by management personnel +1

Changes to the BOM

9.   Who recommends them?

.25 points per example of role (no more than 1 point total earned here)

10. Is there a review and approval process?

Yes / No   Yes = 1.5

11. How detailed is it?

Submit
Reviewed by…
Benefit analysis
Decision

No points

12. Are they reviewed to make standard changes to similar BOMs?

Improvements/changes applied across board within company   +1.5
Improvements/changes applied across board within plant   + 1

Temporary BOMs

13. Are they permitted?

Yes / No   No = 4 (skip to 17), Yes = 0

14. If so, in what cases?

No points

15. With whose authorization?

No points

BOM Accuracy

16. Are BOMs regularly audited for accuracy?

Yes / No   Yes = .5

17. If so, how often?

All records annually   +1
All records every 2 years   +.5

18. Who is accountable for their accuracy?

Qualified role identified+.5

19. Using what method?

Compare actual BOMs vs. actual in plant   +.1

20. With what expected outcome?

>98% BOM accuracy vs. plant actual   +.1
>95% BOM accuracy vs. plant actual   +.5
>90% BOM accuracy vs. plant actual   +.25

BOM Usage

21. What are your BOMs used for? E.g. Parts procurement, standard parts lists, maintenance planning

.25 pts for each use listed that matched those below (up to 1.25)

Purchasing

Equipment representation

Storeroom stock levels

Standard parts lists

Maintenance planning

22. Are they attached/assigned to specific equipment/items in your plant?

Yes / No   Yes = 1.25

23. If so, how?

Clearly attached and easily accessible, electronically
by individual record per equipment   +1.5

Clearly attached and easily accessible, electronically
but not by individual record per equipment   +.1

Clearly attached and easily accessible, by individual
card file per equipment   +.5

Clearly attached and easily accessible, in tech pubs   +.25

24. Is the BOM information shared with other areas of your business and/or company?

Yes / No   Yes = 4

- **Pre-planned maintenance tasks**

A pre-defined template that can be pulled into a work order or maintenance plan, which identifies the work to be conducted, the components needed, the estimated effort required, the frequency of the task, the external resources needed, and any external documents to be used for the task.

Procedures

1. Do you have a standard list of maintenance tasks?

Yes / No   Yes = 2

2. If so what kind?

Preventative

Reactive

Autonomous

Upgrades/Modifications

+.5 for each

3. At what level in your plant's machinery hierarchy are they assigned?

plant,	1
line/process	2
assembly	3
component	4

Standardization

4. Are they standard procedures?

Yes / No   Yes = 1.5

5. If so, to what level, plant wide? Company wide?

Plant wide +1.5

Company wide +2.5

6. How were they developed?

Manufacturer's recommendation	1
Own recommendation through operator experience	2.5
Own recommendation through data analysis program	4

7. Where are they kept?

No points

All in one central place

Organized

8. How accessible are they?

No points

Readily available nearby

Brought with technology to job site

Have to find in publications/drawings

9. What percentage of the work done monthly could be used?

List them

No points

10. What percentage of the monthly work is done using them?

> 90 %	4
80 – 90	3.5
70 – 80	3
60 – 70	2.5

50 – 60   2
35 – 50   1.5
25 – 35   1
10 – 25   .5
0 – 10   0

11. What's in them?

Resources to be used

Parts to be used

Step-by-step instructions

Drawings, etc

+.5 per example up to 3 pts

12. How much detail is in each task description?

No points

13. What kind of frequency is the regular work based on?

No points

Time   E.g. Monthly, weekly

Performance   E.g. Operating hours, revolutions

Other _____ E.g. Six months or 1000 operating hours

Who uses the data?

14. Who uses the pre-planned maintenance task documentation?

Technicians

Planners

Operators

Managers

+.5 per role listed (up to 2 pts)

15. For what purpose?

Planning
To do the work

+ 1 for each

16. What is the official intent of these procedures?

Guidelines for the work   1
Recommended – do what you need to get the work done 2.5
Policy – must follow these steps, use these parts…   4
Other _____

Responsibility

17. Who is responsible for changing/improving them?

1 specific role identified   1.5
2 specific roles identified   .75
>2 specific roles identified   0

18. Is there a process for changing /improving them?

Formal process   1
Informal process   5

19. If so, describe it.

No points

20. How often are changes/improvements made?

No points

21. Are they shared across the plant? the company?

The company   1.5
The plant   .75

- **Work centers**

Group responsible for performing the maintenance work. Can be grouped by any variable including cost center, special skills, line or process, etc...

Structure

1. Are work centers used in your organizational structure?

Yes / No   Yes = .5

2. How were they established?

Based on organizational chart   +.5

3. Who maintains them?

Maintenance, accounting, HR personnel

+.5 pt per group

4. How are they broken down? E.g. By individual, skill type, both ...

Individual or group
Skill set
Accounting

+.5 pt per group

5. How is the work center budgeted?

95% of budget comes from real planning data	4
Planning data and eye-ball estimate	2.5
Eye-ball estimate	1

Planned costs include: planned labor hours, training, vacation, benefits, wages...

6. How often is budgeting performed at the work center level?

No points

Capacity

7. Is their capacity known?

Yes / No   Yes = 1

8. Is capacity data audited regularly for accuracy?

Yes / No   Yes = 1

# of capacities,   total hours, shifts, hours per shift

9. Is it used?

Yes / No   Yes = 1

10. If so for what purpose?

Labor planning
Work leveling

+.5 per answer up to 1 pt

- **Authorization documents**

Documents that are required for approval in order to begin, execute or end a maintenance task.

1. Does any work in your plant require authorization before starting?

No points

2. What kind of work requires authorization and by whom?

No points

Work type   **Approved by**

E.g. Electrical   Lead electrician & maintenance
or production supervisor
Safety
Welding
Start-up

Approval

3. What is the process to plan and execute work which requires authorization?

Authorization obtained 2 days prior	+2
Authorization obtained day before start	.5
Authorization obtained at start	0

4. How is the approval documented?

Online on job ticket	+.5
On job ticket	+.5
Signature required	+2

5. With how much detail?

Name

Date and time of approval

Date & time of authorization to work

+1 1/3 point per item

6.   What kinds of issues limit authorization?

No points

Resource availability?

Costs?

Safety?

Time?

Timing?

7.   How robust is your process to changing environments?

A.   Someone always available on-site for approvals   4

B.   Someone always available via phone for approvals 2.5

C.   Someone available on day shift only   1

D.   Other _____

Over-ride approval

8.   Does your approval process have overrides in special circumstances?

Yes / No   No = 4 (go to 11)

9.   If so, what kinds?

No points

10. Who determines if overrides are acceptable?

1 person of formidable leadership position   2

2 people – one on each 12 hour shift/shift supervisor   1

Any supervisor   0

11. Who's expected to use the process?

Everyone – no exceptions   4

Any exceptions   0

12. Who's responsible for the process?

1 person of formidable leadership position   4

2 people – one on each 12 hour shift/shift supervisor   2.5

Every supervisor   1

13. How are improvements to the process made?

No points

- **Special skills**

The technical ability or aptitude of the person required to complete a task.

Skill assignment

1. Are your special skills identified?

Yes / No   No = 0 (go to next section), Yes = 1

2. If so, how?

No points

3. What are they? E.g. welder, pipefitter, electrician, ….

No points

Welder
Plumber
Pipefitter
Electrician
Mechanic
Toolmaker

4. Are they broken down into levels of expertise as well? E.g.   Beginner, advanced, expert

Yes   +.5

3 levels   +.25

>3 levels   +.5

5. Where are the skills documented?

No points

Personnel file
Badge
Spreadsheet
HR record
Board nearby

6. Who assigns them/qualifies them to the individual?

Qualified supervisor   +1
Qualified technician   +.75
Any supervisor   +.25

7. Are they recognized by the company or trade or is it what a supervisor knows they can do?

Recognized +.1, supervisor's knowledge = 0

8. Who updates/maintains the records?

No points

Work assignment

9. Is this information used when assigning work?

Yes / No   Yes = 2

10. Who uses it?

No points

Maintenance planner
Maintenance supervisor

11. Is capacity planning used to maximize efforts of those skills?

Yes / No   Yes = 2

- **Change management process**

The process to maintain the accuracy of maintenance records in order to reflect current plant structure, record production activity, maintenance events, item performance and cost history.

1. How standard is the database (structural and historical maintenance records) for your company?

A. Each similar line in the same plant is basically the same

B. Each similar line in the same plant is exactly the same, with very few exceptions

C. Each similar line in every plant is basically the same

D. Each similar line in every plant is exactly the same, with very few exceptions

E. Each similar line in the same plant is exactly the same, with no exceptions

F. Each similar line in every plant is exactly the same, with no exceptions

A=.5, B=1, C=1.5, D=3, E=2, F=4

2. What events cause you to make changes to your database?

No points

3. When items are changed/improved such as changing parts list or improving procedures, are those changes reflected in the entire database or in a particular area, plant , or business only?

Entire database   4

Plant wide 2.5

Particular area/

Production line   1

New records

4. How are new records created?

No points

5. By whom?

By trained technicians from good source data   +1.5

6.   In what instances?

+.25 for each instance (up to 1pt)

Changeover, build, teardown…

7.   With what approval?

TDB Admin	1.5
Central maintenance supervisor	.75
Maintenance supervisor	.5

Change request

8.   How are changes recommended?

Formal documentation process – written or electronic	3
Change/improvement meetings – weekly	2
Change/improvement meetings – monthly	1.5
General suggestion	1
Engineer/technician choice	.5

9.   Who can recommend changes?

Specific roles – 0 points

Anyone -   + 1

10. How does one know the status of your recommendation once it is created?

No points

Approval process

11. What is the change approval process?

No points

12. How are changes approved/denied?

Formal change approval process with business wide perspective　　　4
Formal change approval process with plant wide perspective　　2.5
Formal change approval process with production line perspective 1

13. By who?

Qualified representatives from each affected plant　　4
Qualified representatives from within the plant　　2

Change promulgation

14. How are changes promulgated?

No points

15. By who?

No points

Change implementation

16. How are changes implemented?

No points

17. By whom?

No points

18. In what timeframe? (add the two for total)

Major		Minor	
3-6 months	2	0-1 month	2
6-9 months	1	2-4 months	1
9-12 months	.5	4-6 months	.5
12 or > months	0	6 or > months	0

19. How do you know the change is completely implemented?

Follow-up documentation process

No points

20. Who is responsible for these records?

TDB Admin	4
Central maintenance supervisor	2.5
Maintenance supervisor	1

Change audits

21. How are records audited?

Verify equipment records against actuals in plant	1.5

22. By whom?

Knowledgeable, in place audit team	1.25
Knowledgeable assigned personnel, as needed	.75

23. What is done with the results?

Forwarded to management for review and rectify	1.25

24. How often?

All records annually	4
All records every 2 years	2.5
Some randomly, every month	1

25. What are the expected results?

98% or > accuracy	4
95 – 98% accuracy	2.5
90 – 95% accuracy	1

Maintenance Programs

Maintenance Programs

- **Preventative (PM)**

A program consisting of a series of time and/or performance-based maintenance it includes replacements, overhauls and major inspections that are essential to maintain optimal operating conditions.

1. Do you have a formal preventative maintenance program?

Yes / No   Yes = 1

2. Is it documented?

Yes / No   Yes = 1

3. If so, in what format? Please describe.

Broad grouping of data, hardcopy	.5
Specific to the task and maintenance item, hardcopy	1
Broad grouping of data, CMMS	1
Specific to the task and maintenance item, CMMS	2

4. How accessible is the information?

All users can review	4
Planners and supervisors, only	2

5. How are the specific PM tasks identified? E.g. card files, job procedures, etc

Title	1
Title & description	2
Title, description, and procedures	3

Title, description, procedures and specific tools, labor required, and materials   4

Work completion

6.   How is their completion documented and verified?

Noted on work list for the day/week   1.5

Entry into CMMS   3

7.   What data is required?

+.25 per piece of information (up to 1 pt)

Actual parts used, time to complete the work, start and end times, readings, results of work, improvements recommended…

Improvements

8.   How are improvements to the tasks recommended?

Formal documentation process – written or electronic   4

Change/improvement meetings – weekly   3.5

Change/improvement meetings – monthly   2.5

General suggestion   1.5

Engineer/technician choice   1

9.   How quickly are they implemented? (add the two for the total)

Major		Minor	
3-6 month s	2	0-1 month	2
6-9 month s	1	2-4 months	1
9-12 months	.5	4-6 months	.5
12 or > months	0	6 or > months	0

10. How widespread is the implementation?

Entire company database	4
Plant wide	2.5
Particular area	/
production line	1

- **Autonomous (AM)**

Equipment monitoring or basic maintenance requiring little or no downtime and only consumable components in order to keep the plant operating efficiently. Usually performed by operating personnel.

1. Do you have a formal autonomous maintenance program?

Yes / No   Yes = 1

2. Is it documented?

Yes / No   Yes = 1

3. If so, in what format? Please describe.

Broad grouping of data, hardcopy	.5
Specific to the task and maintenance item, hardcopy	1
Broad grouping of data, CMMS	1
Specific to the task and maintenance item, CMMS	2

4. How accessible is the information?

All users can review	4
Planners and supervisors only	2

5. How are the specific PM tasks identified? E.g. card files, job procedures, etc

Title	1
Title & description	2
Title, description, and procedures	3
Title, description, procedures and specific tools, labor required, and materials	4

Work completion

6. How is their completion documented and verified?

84

Noted on work list for the day/week   1.5

Entry into CMMS   3

7.   What data is required?

+.25 per piece of information (up to 1 pt)

Actual parts used, time to complete the work, start and end times, readings, results of work, improvements recommended…

Improvements

8.   How are improvements to the tasks recommended?

Formal documentation process – written or electronic	4	
Change/improvement meetings – weekly		3.5
Change/improvement meetings – monthly	2.5	
General suggestion	1.5	
Engineer/technician choice	1	

9.   How quickly are they implemented? (add the two for the total)

Major		Minor	
3-6 month s	2	0-1 month	2
6-9 month s	1	2-4 months	1
9-12 months	.5	4-6 months	.5
12 or > months	0	6 or > months	0

10. How widespread is the implementation?

Entire company database	4
Plant wide	2.5
Particular area	/
production line	1

Reactive and condition-based (RM & CBM)

All non-preventative maintenance work which emerges from day-to-day business operations. There are two types:

1) Emergency/breakdown - which directly effect reliability and must be corrected immediately

2) Planned - which permits time to plan and schedule the work into the integrated production/maintenance schedule. This work includes projects, business initiatives, safety items, and condition-based items which may involve maintenance resources

1. Do you have a formal reactive maintenance program to deal with unplanned maintenance events?

Yes / No   Yes = 1

2. Is it documented?

Yes / No   Yes = 1

3. If so, in what format? Please describe.

Broad grouping of data, hardcopy	.5
Specific to the task and maintenance item, hardcopy	1
Broad grouping of data, CMMS	1
Specific to the task and maintenance item, CMMS	2

4. How accessible is the information?

All users can review	4
Planners and supervisors only	2

5. How are the specific PM tasks identified? E.g. card files, job procedures, etc

Title	1
Title & description	2
Title, description, and procedures	3

Title, description, procedures and specific tools, labor required, and materials   4

Work completion

6.   How is their completion documented and verified?

Noted on work list for the day/week   1.5
Entry into CMMS   3

7.   What data is required?

+.25 per piece of information (up to 1 pt)
Actual parts used, time to complete the work, start and end times, readings, results of work, improvements recommended…

Improvements

8.   How are improvements to the tasks recommended?

Formal documentation process – written or electronic   4
Change/improvement meetings – weekly   3.5
Change/improvement meetings – monthly   2.5
General suggestion   1.5
Engineer/technician choice   1

9.   How quickly are they implemented? (add the two for the total)

	Major		Minor
3-6 months	2	0-1 month	2
6-9 months	1	2-4 months	1
9-12 months	.5	4-6 months	.5
12 or > months	0	6 or > months	0

10. How widespread is the implementation?

Entire company database   4

Plant wide	2.5
Particular area	/
production line	1

- **Backlogs**

List of outstanding tasks to be performed which do not have a specific completion data planned.

1. Do you regularly maintain a backlog of maintenance work?

If no, no backlog, all is planned – assign a 4 for this section and move to next one

Yes , and it is maintained   2
No, have one but not maintained   1

2. If so, how is it created?

Work comes up and is added immediately to backlog
Planned and scheduled work is missed and added to backlog

No points

3. Are there any formal plans to get the work done?

The operative word here is formal

No points

4. If so, on average, how soon?

For reactive, non-emergency

<10 days from when item was added to backlog 4
10 – 20 days   2
20 – 30 days   1

No points for any other work that missed its scheduled date and is added to backlog E.g. PMs

5. Please list the reasons you would put a job in the backlog. E.g. lack of parts, time, labor, etc.

No points

6.   What is the percentage of orders in the backlog for each of the above reasons?

No points

7.   What percentage of your maintenance work comes from the backlog?

0	4
1-5.1	3.5
5-10	3
10-25	2
25-50	1
25-51	

Maintenance Planning and Execution

Maintenance Planning

- ### Planning, scheduling, and capacity utilization

Maintenance work can come from many sources and includes all PMs, reactive and emergency items. Maintenance planning and scheduling provides maintenance planners the data to know

- who and what is needed
- when and where
- for how long
- how many

and allows planners to optimize the utilization of every resource.

1. Is there an overall maintenance plan for your plant/site?

Yes / No   No points

2. What is the long and short-term importance to the following levels of your company's organizational structure?

Line/process
Plant
Company

No points

3. How consistent are the details of the overall maintenance plan with what is actually accomplished in the day-to-day operations of your plant?

95% or more of actuals = daily plans   +4
90-95   3.5

80-90 %	3
70-80	2.5
60-70	2
50-60	1.5
35-50	1
25-35	.5

4. Who is responsible for the overall maintenance plan?

One planner full-time	+4
Each supervisor	2.5
Work center leaders/technicians	1

5. Who creates and maintains the plan?

One planner full-time	+4
Each supervisor	2.5
Work center leaders/technicians	1

6. Who can change the plan (not its execution)?

Only full-time planner or officially designated rep	+4

7. Under what circumstances and with what authorization?

No circumstances	+4
Emergency/breakdown only	4
Production need	2

8. What is included in the plan? (.75 points per item, no more than 4pts total)

Parts required	labor
Special tools	documentation
External services	costs

9. Is it linked to anything?

Yes / No

10. If so, what? (.5 points per item)

Material management

Purchasing

Capacity planning

MRP

Manufacturing

Financials

Human resources/payroll

Technical history

11. What level of your organizational structure is your overall maintenance plan broken down to?

Individual	4
Lowest work group	3
Highest work group	2
Site/plant	1

12. Is there a separate plan for each line/process?

Yes +4   / No

13. Is it a subset of the overall plan?

Yes +4

No   It's separate and more detailed = 0

14. At what level of detail?

High level – approximate schedule, no requirements	+1
Medium level – firm schedule, big ticket requirements, costs long lead items	2.5
Low level – firm schedule, all requirements	4

15. How far in advance of the actual work are the detailed plans made?

Detailed = job by job with resource requirements

1 year or more   4

9-12 months   3

6-9 months   2.5

3-6 months   1.5

1-3 months   1

<1 month .   5

16. Are the plans firm?

Firm = not changeable without authorization (see #7)

30 or > days   4

21-30 days   3

14-21 days   2.5

7-14 days   2

week of   1

day before   .5

day of   0

17. Are maintenance planning decisions data-based, with pre-defined business goals and steps to achieve the goals?

No points

18. How is the overall maintenance plan integrated with the other parts of your plant?
E.g. Purchasing, production, and storeroom

+1 1/3 per matching answer

Relayed to them & integrated with their plan

Leveraged purchasing

Set inventory levels

Production Labor integration

19. Is production personnel labor made available for maintenance (when not in production)?

Yes (+ 1) /   No

20. To what extent is the amount known?

Exactly   + 1
Approximately   + .5
Not known   0

21. Is it used as part of your plans?

Yes (+1   )   /   No

22. If so, how?

Formally integrated with the overall maintenance plan   +1
Used as time becomes available (informally)   .5

Sharing maintenance planning data

23. Are maintenance planning data and requirements shared with production planners?

Yes (+1.5) /   No

24. If so, how?

Formally   +1
Informally   0

25. Do you produce an integrated maintenance and production schedule for the plant?

Yes (+1.5) /   No

26. At what level of detail?

High level – approximate schedule, no requirements   +1

Medium level – firm schedule, big ticket requirements, costs long lead items   2.5

Low level – firm schedule, all requirements   4

27. How far in advance of the actual work are the detailed plans made?

Detailed = job by job with resource requirements

1 year or more   4

9-12 months   3

6-9 months   2.5

3-6 months   1.5

1-3 months   1

<1 month   .5

28. Are the plans firm?

Firm = not changeable without authorization (see #7)

30 or > days   4

21-30 days   3

14-21 days   2.5

7-14 days   2

week of   1

day before   .5

day of   0

Production and Maintenance meetings

29. Are there regular meetings to discuss long and short-term plans in detail?

Yes (+1)   /   No

30. If so, how often?

Daily or more	+1.5
2 or 3 times a week	1
weekly	.5
> weekly	.25

31. What is discussed?

+.5 per each

schedule

resource availability

long & short-term issues

32. If the schedule is discussed, how far in advance? (4 points maximum)

	+1.5	1	.5	.25
Days of low level detail	30	20	10	5
Days of mid level detail	90	60	30	20
Days of high level detail	180	90	60	30

Production and Maintenance Integration

33. Does one area drive the other or do they work together to create a common plan?

Yes (+1.5) /   No

34. Is an agreement between maintenance and production required for the resultant schedule?

Yes (+1)   /   No

35. If so, what kind?

Mutual   +1.5

Production driven   0

Maintenance driven   0

36. Is there any other formal contact between the two departments?

No points

37. What kinds, how often?

No points

38. How productive?

No points

Resources in plan

39. Are resources included in the plan?

Yes (+1)   /   No

40. If so, what kind? (+.75 points for each that matches)

Labor, parts, special equipment, vendor assistance

Resource availability review

41. Is resource availability checked?

Yes (+1)   /   No

42. If so, how?

Online internally and with vendor   +2

Online and manually with vendor   1.5

Manager's appointment book   1

Manager's recollection   .5

43. Is work center capacity part of your maintenance plan?

Yes (+1) / No

44. What time frame is capacity tracked?

Hours   4

Daily   3

Weekly   2

Monthly   1

45. How often is it calculated?

Daily   4

Weekly   2.5

Monthly   1.5

In special circumstances, such as major outages   1

Work center capacity accuracy

46. How accurately do you account for work center capacity?

Finitely determined as changes are made – if this answer + 2

47. Are personnel vacations tracked as part of available capacity?

Yes (+.5) /   No

48. Are sick days?

Yes (+.5) /   No

49. Are holidays?

Yes (+.5) /   No

50. Is training?

Yes (+.5) /   No

51. What makes up the total capacity available to do maintenance work?

Total number of employees and their total number of effort hours available
- if this answer then + 2

52. How are these numbers used?

Integral part of the high level site work plan   +1
Integral part of the low level site work plan   +1
Integral part of the short-term meetings to
allocate resources in advance of the work   +.5
Integral part of supervisors' decisions, day maintenance
is due to allocated work +.5

53. Is there a role specifically assigned to maximize the work and the available resources?

Yes (+4)   /   No

54. Are the resource requirements of your pre-planned tasks used to help determine the overall resource requirements for the plan?

Yes /   No   no points

Lead times

55. Do material lead times play a part in your maintenance plans?

Yes (+2)   /   No

56. What other factors can impact your plans?

Availability and lead times for contractors

Special tools/resources off-site

Special tools on-site

Own labor capacity

+.5 per each matching answer

Plan accuracy

57. Is there a role responsible for reviewing the work for completion and accuracy?

Yes (+1.5) /   No

58. If so, how accurate is the information coming from the pre-planned tasks?

Modified

0-5%	+2.5
5-10	2
10-20%	1.5
20-30%	1
30-40	.5
>40%	0

59. Are provisions made within your plans to deal with reactive maintenance and how it impacts the schedule?

Yes /   No   no points

60. Have scheduling response parameters (firm zones) been pre-established in writing?

Yes (+4)   /   No

61. For what parts of your business?

One and 1/3 point for each answer

Production, purchasing, maintenance

62. What is the size of firm zone?

0-10 days	1
10-20 days	2.5
20-30 days	4

63. What can/can't be changed within the firm zone?

Schedule – no

Requirements – yes – if no longer needed or wrong

+2 per matching answer

Individual schedule control

64. By whom?

Planners and their supervisors only +2

65. With what authorization/concurrence?

With concurrence of maintenance/production planner/supervisor counterparts +2

66. How is it upheld?

No points

67. What if the firm zone is violated?

No points

68. How often is it not upheld?

Always upheld   +4

Upheld 90% of the time   2

Upheld <90% of the time   0

69. What is the overall maintenance planning, scheduling, and firm zone process?

No points

70. What are outside effects and how do they impact the outcome of your plan?

No points

Leadership

71. Does a leadership team agree with the plan and sign it regularly?

Yes (+2)   /   No

72. Who makes up this team?

+.5 per matching answer

Plant/site manager

Superintendents of maintenance and production

Lead supervisors

Planners

Feedback

73. Is there a method to provide feedback for scheduling improvements?

Yes (+2)   /   No

74. Formal or informal?

Formal   +2
Informal   0

75. When the plan is complete, who is the information shared with and how?

No points

76. Who takes action from it?

All plant personnel   no points

77. Are changes permitted to your plans?

No points

78. How often do these changes happen?

0-5%   +4
5-10   3
10-15   2.5
15-20   1.5
20-25   1
25-30   .5

79. What kinds of changes routinely occur in your plan?

No points

80. How often are parts added to or substituted in the original plan?

0-3%   +4
4-6   3
7-9   2.5
10-12   2
13-15   1.5

16-18	1
19-22	.5

81. How often is capacity overloaded?

0-3%	+4
4-7	3
7-10	2.5
10-13	2
13-16	1.5
16-19	1
19-22	.5

82. Are there any work backlogs?

0%	4
1-5	3
5-10	2
10-15	1

83. How often is the expediting of parts/resources performed?

0%	4
1-5	3
5-11	2
10-15	1

- **Priority systems**

A method of determining level of precedence among work requirements. It can assist with order planning, scheduling, and allocation of resources for task completion.

1. Is there a formal, in-writing work priority system in place?

If no, assign a score of 0 for this section and move on to the next area

2. If so, are there more than one?

Yes /   No   no points

3. Please describe them.

No points

4. How many priority levels in each system?

No points

5. Who assigns them?

The individual that plans the work +4

6. How objectively is the priority set for each job?

Formal priority system is used   4
Based on planner's ability to gauge the priority rules & work requests   1.5
Based on immediate need   0

7. How often is it used?

Always   4
95% of the time   3
90-95%   2

<90%   1

8. Is the priority system used when planning the maintenance work?

Yes (+4)   /   No

9. If so, how? Please give an example.

No points

10. Are there any over-riding factors which, once a priority is set, could change the priority or the originally scheduled date of a maintenance task?

Yes /   No   no points

11. If so, what kinds and with whose authorization are changes made?

Emergency, safety, breakdown are acceptable kinds when authorization is made by the planner/supervisor and with production agreement = 4

Otherwise = 0

12. How well is the system adhered to in the day-to-day operations of your plant?

98% or better   +4
95-98 %   3.5
90-95   3
85-90   2
80-85   1
75-80   0

13. Does it include PMs?

No = 4

Explain: PMs should not be prioritized because that shows you have an option if and when to complete them. It doesn't mean they can't slide some on the schedule, but your work process should be that they are in the firm zone. PMs should be a baseline of maintenance commitment which is held in place to maximize equipment reliability. Reactive maintenance, in many cases, is a result of inconsistent PM programs. Thus a good, proven PM program should be the baseline of maintenance performed on your equipment.

- **Performing the work**

Execution of the maintenance task including completing the follow-up documentation.

1. How is work promulgated to the technician?

No points

White board, electronic print out, face to face, as necessary – they find out on their own
Phone, walkie-talkie

2. How is this documented?

CMMS	4
Spreadsheet on computer	3
White board/bulletin board/note pad	2
Time card only record of what was done	1

3. What if last minute changes to the job are needed, how is the technician notified about the change?

Update with new paperwork	4
Verbally	1

4. How is this documented?

No points

5. How often are there last minute changes (day of job)?

0-5%	+4
5-10	3
10-15	2.5
15-20	1.5
20-25	1
25-30	.5

6. How detailed is the job data provided to the technicians?

.75 per item that match

procedures, drawings (when applicable), parts list, tools list

7. Are skills required listed in the jobs?

Yes (+4)   /   No

8. Are permits/authorizations reviewed before any work starts?

Yes (+4)   /   No

9. What other data resources are available to the technician to help with maintenance tasks?

No points

10. How accessible is this information to the technician?

Every technician has it readily available on-line   4
Can make request for additional information   2.5
They have to find it themselves   1

11. Is the accuracy of the work plan validated before the job starts?

Yes (+4)   /   No

Plan validation

12. If so, how?

Review labor, parts, tools, procedures (+.75 for each)

13. By whom?

Supervisor/Lead technician   +1

14. What if a problem is found before the job starts? E.g. Wrong parts, required skills not available, no technical drawings - how is it resolved?

Planner/scheduler works to resolve problem for technician   4

Technician/supervisor resolves problem   2.5

Technician starts work and resolves it/works around it as they go   1

15. Who can make the decision to reschedule or alter a job?

Planner/scheduler/supervisor   if 2 of 3   4

Technician   1.5

16. Once a job is started, if additional resources are required and not on the list, how are they obtained?

Planner/scheduler/supervisor resolves it   4

Other   0

17. How is this documented?

Additions to the original work plan document   4

No documentation   0

18. If additional work is found, how is it processed?

Document and feed plan to planner/scheduler to resolve   4

Do work, no document   0

19. How does it impact the overall maintenance plan?

Worked into the current overall maintenance plan
reviewing the priority and availability of resources   4

No impact – put in backlog   0

20. Once the job is completed, what is documented by the technician?

Time – start, complete, effort hours

Materials used

Continuous improvement inputs

Who did the work

+1 per match, up to 4

21. Where is it recorded?

CMMS	4
Spreadsheet on computer	3
White board/bulletin board/note pad	2
Time card only record of what was done	1

22. Where is it stored?

CMMS	4
Electrical files on computer	2.5
File cabinets	1
Not saved > 90 days	0

23. How is task completion tracked?

CMMS	4
Spreadsheet on computer	3
White board/bulletin board/note pad	2
Time card only record of what was done	1

24. How is it verified?

Supervisor/lead technician/QA reviews work	4
No review	0

25. Can inputs be provided to improve procedures, parts lists, etc?

Yes (+4)   /   No

26. If so, how?

On work ticket   4
On separate form   3
Verbally   1.5

27. Is it part of a formal improvement process?

Yes (+4)   /   No

28. Are there formal maintenance history requirements?

Yes (+4)   /   No

29. If so, from where?

No points

- **Reporting**

Reviewing the records in the maintenance database for specific details to better understand the business

1. What reports are used in your business?

Name	Frequency	Who	Importance
E.g. parts usage by line	bi-monthly	maint planner	#1 factor in line costs

Parts usage data

Problem reporting

Technical history

Life cycle costing of equipment

Breakdown data

Reviewing your PM program

Trend analysis

Budgeting

Job cost planning – plans vs. actuals

+.5 per matching answer, up to 4 total

+.5 point for each report which is run at least monthly

2. Which are most important to maintenance personnel?

No points

3. Who uses this data?

Planners, supervisors, engineering, accounting

+1 per matching answer

4. To do what?

Continuous improvement

Review planned vs. actuals

Review costs

Review labor

+1 per matching answer

5. How are your business reports generated?

Online, in CMMS   4
Manually with spreadsheets   2

6. By who?

No points

7. How often?

No points

8. In what format?

A. Hard copy?   1
B. Created on-line   2.5
C. Created on-line, real time   4

9. What is done with this data to make business decisions?

<u>RoleReport nameDecision</u>

No points

- **Budgeting**

The estimate of the total costs for a maintenance department or work center. It includes the number of personnel required and all of their associated expenses.

1. How often is your budget reviewed in your company?

No points

2. What is the lowest budget level?

A. Plant   1
B. Work center 4
C. Line/process 2.5

3. How much detail is required? Please give specific line items

Direct labor   Meetings/administrative
Overtime   Benefits
Vacation   Training
Travel

+ 2/3 point per matching answer, up to 4

4. How are the budget numbers generated?

A. From previous history/past performance – combined with future view   2.5
B. Completely from future work plans   4
C. Mostly from past performance   1

5. Who creates the budgets for each level?

No points

6. Who submits the budget?

No points

7. Who approves it?

No points

8. What is done with this data when finally approved?

No points

9. Are actuals vs. planned budget numbers tracked?

Yes (+4)   /   No

10. How?

Monthly comparison of line/work center planned vs. actuals   +4

11. By whom?

No points

12. What are the impacts if over or under the planned budget?

No points

13. How does it affect local plans?

Should not cut maintenance if over budget

If that is the answer next 3 sections are 0 points of 3

14. … the overall plant strategy?

See above

15. … the overall company strategy?

See above

Material Planning

<u>Material planning</u>

- **Output of planning systems and ability to meet needs**

Integrating the maintenance work planning systems with the material planning systems and sharing data to determine and meet material needs

1. How do you determine future maintenance spare parts needs?

Historical Usage
Future plans
Stock levels

+1 1/3 for each

2. Are material needs identified in advance of the work by the maintenance plan?

Yes (+4) / No

3. What data comes from the plan?

part number
amount
when needed
manufacturer..
where material is needed

+1 for each up to 4 points total

4. What is the average lead time for parts?

No points

5. How far in advance are parts received for use into the storeroom?

0 working days	3 points
1-3 working days	3.5 points
3-5 working days	4 points
5-10 working days	3 points
> 10 working days	2 points

6. Is lead time used to purchase parts in a leveraged manner?

Yes +4 / No

7. What percentage of parts are long lead items (more than 30 days)?

No points

8. How far in advance of the planned work date are parts requested by the technician/planner?

List the percentages accordingly

0 working days
1-3 working days
3-5 working days
5-10 working days
10-20 working days
20-30 working days
>30 working days

If 90% of the work is >30 days	+4
If 75% of the work is >30 days	+3.5
If 60% of the work is >30 days and >20% of the work is 20-30 days	+3
If 50% of the work is >30 days and >20% of the work is 10-20 days	+2.5
If 40% of the work is >30 days and >20% of the work is 20-30 days	+2

If 30% of the work is >30 days and >20 % of the work is 10-20 days   +1.5

If 30% of the work is >30 days and >20% of the work is 5-10 days   + 1

If 20% of the work is >30 days   +.5

9. Do material firm zones exist?

Material firm zones are set up to firm up frames where once the work plans and requirements are entered, they are "rigidly" in place and must meet certain requirements in order to be changed. E.g. No changes are to be made in their schedule in the final five days before any maintenance task unless caused by an emergency or safety event.

Yes +4 / No

10. If so, are they clearly defined in writing?

Yes +4 / No

11. How well are they adhered to?

Upheld >90% of the time   4

Upheld 80-90% of the time   3

Upheld 70-80% of the time   2

Upheld 60-70% of the time   1

12. Are material lead times taken into consideration when ordering parts by the technician?

Yes +4 / No

13. If so, how?

No points

Lead times affect local plans

Purchasing uses MRP to order JIT

14. Are materials ordered correctly from the maintenance plan?

Yes / No

No points

15. What percentage?

100%	4
98-100%	3.5
95-98%	3
90-95%	2.5
85-90%	2
80-85%	1.5
75-80%	1
70-75%	.5

16. Are materials received on the date requested?

Yes / No

No points

17. If not, what percentage of monthly receipts are on time or early?

100%	4
98-100%	3.5
95-98%	3
90-95%	2.5
85-90%	2
80-85%	1.5
75-80%	1
70-75%	.5

18. Are materials received correctly from supplier?

Yes / No

No points

19. What percentage of monthly receipts are received correctly?

100%   4
98-100%   3.5
95-98%   3
90-95%   2.5
85-90%   2
80-85%   1.5
75-80%   1
70-75%   .5

20. Do you have to expedite parts to fill maintenance work requests?

Yes / No

No points

21. How often?

0% 4
0-2%   3.5
2-5%   3
5-10%   2.5
10-15%   2
15-20%   1.5
20-25%   1
25-30%   .5

22. Why is expediting required? Complete the following chart:

Reason for expediting   % overall expedite requests per month

No points

23. Are materials kitted correctly by storeroom personnel?

Yes / No

No points

24. What percentage are error free?

100%	4
98-100%	3.5
95-98%	3
90-95%	2.5
85-90%	2
80-85%	1.5
75-80%	1
70-75%	.5

25. Are materials delivered to the work site?

Yes / No

No points

26. If so, are they delivered correctly, on time, and ready for use?

Correctly
100%	1.5
95-99%	1
90-95%	.5

On time
100%	1.5
95-99%	1
90-95%	.5

Add one additional point if ready for use

Maximum total =4

27. Do you use outside services and special tools for your maintenance work?

Yes / No

No points

28. If so, how often?

No points

29. What kind of work are they used for?

No points

30. What is your process for requesting these services or tools?

Same as purchasing required materials   +4
Someone/non-purchasing calls to make arrangements   +1.5

31. Who is authorized to make these requests?

+1 point per matching answer

Technician makes the request
Supervisor approves
Purchasing buys them
Supervisor signs off on their use/delivery successfully

- **Supplier involvement**

The level of involvement between a company and its suppliers in determining inventory.

1. Are suppliers involved in setting material lead times?

Yes +4 / No

2. Are they provided with the requirements of your material planning from your plant?

Yes +4 / No

3. If so at what level of operation?

For a …
Line/process   +2
Plant   +3
Company   +4

4. How have inventories been affected for the factory and supplier?

No points

5. Are there clear policies are established to resolve problems with suppliers?

Yes +4 / No

6. If so, what are they?

No points

7. Are clear points of contact established by each plant and supplier to resolve them?

Yes +4 / No

- **Stock usage, safety stock, leveraged purchasing**

Understanding the stock requirements from planned and unplanned maintenance tasks and developing a formula for determining safety stock levels. That formula can be rolled into the overall material plan to enable grouped purchasing for the site/company.

1. Is there a written part procurement process in place?

Yes +4 / No

2. If so, please describe it here.

No points

3. How is the request processed between the storeroom and purchasing personnel?

Automatically using MRP	4
Automatically using a computer	3
Requests entered into computer – processed not using MRP	2
All on paper	1

4. What steps must the request go through before it is approved?

Supervisor level approval on all parts within manufacturing/maintenance 4

5. How is this documented?

In system	4
On paper, no system	2

6. Where do the costs go?

Specific order/work request	4
To department/line/process level	3
To business area level	2
To plant level	1

7. How is the costing documented?

In system, linked to financial systems	4
In system, not linked to financial systems	3
On paper, no system	2

8. Once a part is identified as needed (from planned or reactive maintenance), who can make the request for the part?

No points

9. Where is the request made?

Via a parts processing system	4
On a computer list – not linked to purchasing system	2
On paper	1

10. How does the request come into the storeroom?

Via a parts processing system	4
On a computer list – not linked to purchasing system	2
On paper	1

11. How much lead time does the storeroom usually get to provide the part?

Days in advance Percentage of parts used per month
0 - 3
3 – 7
7 – 14
14 – 30
30 or more

No points

12. Are parts reserved within your storeroom?

Yes +4 / No

13. If so, how?

In system	4
On paper, no system	2

14. Where are they stored until used?

At location (line/process) where they are needed until use	4
At bins in storeroom	3

15. What identifies them as being for a particular maintenance job?

Order/work task/linked back to the specific task	4
When they are issued to the order	1.5

16. If reactive maintenance occurs and you need a reserved part to fix the problem, is there a procedure to resolve who gets the available part?

Yes +4 / No

17. If so, what is it?

No points

18. Is there a set of priorities in place assigned to each request which helps determine who gets the part?

Yes +4 / No

19. If so, what is it?

No points

20. Is it in writing?

Yes +4 / No

21. Is it promulgated?

No points

22. Who makes the priority decision?

No points

23. Is anyone else involved?

No points

24. Do you make your own parts?

Yes / No

No points

25. Who can ask for them?

No points

26. Who approves?

Supervisor level approval on all parts within manufacturing/maintenance 4

27. How is the request documented?

Via a parts processing system	4
On a computer list – not linked to purchasing system	2
On paper	1

28. How is the approval documented?

Via a parts processing system   4

On a computer list – not linked to purchasing system   2

On paper   1

29. Where are the costs of making the part accounted for?

Specific to the request for the part   4

Into a cost collector for all parts manufactured   2

Overhead   1

30. Where do most parts for maintenance work come from? What percentages?

E.g. Stock, POs, nearby authorized spaces, toolboxes, inventory, tool boxes

Resource location   Percentage

No points

31. How are these parts replenished when used?

MRP   4

Ordered for each job, not MRP   3

When inventory is done   2

When requested   1

32. Are there safety stock levels set?

Yes +4 / No

33. If so, how are they determined?

Past history based on data, lead times, requirements/turnover   4

Past history based on someone's experience   1.5

34. By whom?

No points

35. How often are they updated?

Quarterly or more often	4
Annually or more often	3
Only as needed	1

36. Is spare part purchasing leveraged?

Yes +4 / No

37. If so how?

Storeroom operator experience	1
Based on actual requirements from plans	4
Based on historical usages	3

38. What happens if go below safety stock?

Auto-reorder	4
Re-order enough with next requirement	2
Re-order enough at next inventory	1

39. What if the safety stock level is taken to zero, are there special emergency parts procurement procedures?

Yes +4 / No

40. What are they?

No points

- **Parts inventory process**

Identifying which parts and how many of each is on hand and in what location at a plant.

1. Where is your stock held?

No points

2. Is it in a centralized storeroom or system of storerooms?

Centralized +4

3. If there is a system of storerooms, is there a database that is shares a list of all the parts in inventory at all storeroom locations?

If there is a database that shares the inventory information +4

4. Is there a system that displays such things as part location, amount on hand, etc?

Yes +4 / No

5. How accessible is it?

The information is available to..
Floor level personnel, supervisors, material personnel   4
Only supervisors and material personnel   2.5
Only material personnel   1

6. How accurate is the data in the system?

98-100 % accurate   4
95-98%   3
92-95%   2
90-92%   1

7. How often is the accuracy of these records checked?

Quarterly or more frequently   4

Semi-Annually   3

Annually   2

Every 18 months   1

8. By who?

No points

9. Who's responsible for maintaining the accuracy of the storeroom counts?

No points

Check on parts availability

10. Is there any way to check on what's parts are coming in?

Yes +1 / No

11. Is it electronic or manual?

Electronic +3

12. Can one check on what's reserved?

Yes +1 / No

13. Is it electronic or manual?

Electronic +3

14. Can one check on what's ready for pick-up/delivery?

Yes +1 / No

15. Is it electronic or manual?

Electronic +3

16. Is there a policy which determines where parts are kept?

No points

- **Parts delivery process (to work area)**

Bringing the parts required for a maintenance task from the storeroom to the maintenance area.

1. How do parts get to the work area?

Location and delivery date on the work order, used to deliver to work area or storage bin at work area +4

Picked up at storeroom by technician – if this is the answer, assign 0 to this section and move on

2. Who's responsible for this task?

No points

Receipt delivery

3. Is there someone from maintenance or production that receives the part to the work area/bin?

Yes +1 / No

4. Are the items verified for accuracy upon receipt?

Yes +1 / No

5. Are the items tagged to identify the job they are required for?

Yes +1 / No

6. Is this receipt documented?

Yes +1 / No

7. If so, how?

No points

8. How often are the deliveries made?

9.

Every shift	4
Daily for all jobs	3
When required, less frequently than daily	2
Weekly	1

Measures

<u>Measures</u>

- **Success Measures**

Statistics which can gauge the overall performance of a line/process or business.

1. List the specific measures in place to assess the success of your company or business.

<u>Measure</u>   <u>Expected results</u>   <u>Frequency</u>   <u>Who measures</u>

No points

2. How are these goals set?

Business leadership
Past performance

No points

3. What steps are taken if the goals are not achieved?

Shortfalls recognized with a plan of action to correct them	4
Shortfalls noted with reasons for them	2.5
Shortfalls noted	1
None	0

4. Who is responsible for managing your measurement program?

Yes (+4) / No

5. Are comparisons made across lines/processes and/or plants?
Yes (+4) / No

- **Data analysis & continuous improvement**

Reviewing the records in the maintenance database for specific details as outlined in the reporting document to better understand the business and make improvements

1. Once historical data is collected, is there a formal data analysis or continuous improvement program that uses this data?

Yes (+4)   /   No – skip this section and assign a score of zero

2. How is the data collected?

No points

3. What do they do with the information?

Review/analyze – look for trends, problems
Make improvements to product process
Implement within company

+1 per match, up to 4

4. Who performs this data analysis?

Engineering
Continuous improvement team

No points

5. How often?

Monthly or more   4
Quarterly   3
Annually   2

As needed > 1 year   1

6.   What is reviewed/tracked?

Parts usage data

Problem reporting

Technical history

Life cycle costing of equipment

Breakdown data

Reviewing your PM program

Trend analysis

Budgeting

Job cost planning – plans vs. actuals

+.5 per matching answer, up to 4 total

7.   How long is the equipment history kept?

5 or more years   4

4 years   3

3 years   2

2 years or less   1

8.   What are the goals of your continuous improvement program?

Cost savings

More efficient processes

Better product

+1 1/3 per matching answer

9.   Who is involved in the continuous improvement program?

Engineering/design, planner/scheduler, supervisor, technician

+ 1 per matching answer

10. If your company has multiple sites, does your continuous improvement program have representation from all of them?

Yes (+4)   /   No

11. What is done with the results of their review?

Team recommends improvement
Approved for implementation
Plan development for implementation

+1 1/3 per matching answer

12. How quickly?

1 – 3 months   4
4 – 6 months   3
7 – 9 months   2
9 – 12 months   1

How widespread?

13. Are they plant wide?

Yes (+2)   /   No

14. Company wide?

Yes (+2)   /   No

Organizational Effectiveness

<u>Organizational effectiveness</u>

- **Organizational structure**

The representation of how personnel are organized within a plant

1. What are the specific roles or job titles in your maintenance organization?

No points

2. What is the description of each role, including their position in the organization and their authority/responsibility to the overall success or the plant and company? (Please complete on a separate sheet of paper)

No points

3. Are the roles defined in writing?

Yes (+4) / No

4. If so, where?

No points

5. Are the descriptions easily accessible?

No points

6. Are the personnel in these roles trained on these job requirements?

Trained on specific role assigned   4
Trained by paygrade, but not role   2

142

7. At a minimum the following responsibilities exist – who do you have performing these tasks?

If responsibility doesn't match role, enter N/A

No points

Role

- Maintenance planning & scheduling

Long-term maintenance planning

Short-term maintenance planning

Outages

AM program – day to day

PM program - preventative

RM - reactive

Condition-based maintenance program

Documenting measuring points/readings

Role

- Technical work

Repairs to line/process

Repair shop

Supervisor for line/process

Supervisor for repair shop

- Continuous improvement/data analysis/reporting

Reporting

Budgeting

Data analysis

Continuous improvement program

- Overall maintenance leadership

Integration with other business areas

Weekly and monthly production meetings

Work hour by hour issues with production, others

Verify orders are ready to start

- Reactive maintenance work processes

Identify work

Plan work

Set priorities

Resolve emergencies

- Capacity planning of work center

Resource availability decisions

Make personnel assignments

- Documenting work was complete

Follow-up paperwork

Q-A work was performed to standard

Identify additional work that resulted

- Manage materials

Maintaining and periodically reviewing all maintenance

Material parameters such as order quantities, lot sizes, lead times, safety stocks, etc

- Obtain parts and services

Order parts and services

Approve parts and services

Receive parts

Verify services were performed

Verify materials arrive/on track

Prepare materials for each specific job

Deliver/get materials for the job

- Maintain technical documents and drawings
- Maintain database records

8. Are these responsibilities written in their job description?

Yes (+4) / No

9. Are your people rewarded/recognized for achievement?

Yes (+4) / No

10. If so, please describe in detail.

No points

11. Does the reward system in place recognize people for meeting company business goals?

Yes (+4) / No

12. Do they emphasize planning instead of crisis management?

Yes (+4) / No

13. If so, how are they rewarded and in what instances?

No points

14. In your organization, would you say, training is a one-time thing or continuous for all levels of employees?

Continuous, annually, on how to do the job	4
One time per promotion	2.5
Only during time of indoctrination, promotion to management, and upper-management	1
One time at indoctrination	0

15. How are its lessons re-enforced in the workplace?

Continuously updated in a recurring training program

Supervisors one-on-one re-enforcement

Signs on wall in work place

+1 per event up to 4 pts

16. Is there is a formal and ongoing process to identify individual employee improvement opportunities and continuous training?

No points

17. Does management's attitude and actions demonstrate a commitment to fully educate and train people prior to implementing new technologies and processes?

Yes (+4) / No

18. Is the training and education program based on the principles of behavior-change in an organization rather than transferring information regarding a specific technology or advancement? Please give a specific example.

No points

19. Is there an overall company business strategy?

Yes (+4) / No

20. Is there one at the plant level to meet and/or exceed the company's goals?

Yes (+4) / No

21. Is this supported by local managers in actions and words?

Yes (+4) / No

22. Does each person known what their part is to achieve the company and plant overall goals?

Yes (+4) / No

23. Is it documented?

Yes (+4) / No

24. How easily is this information accessible?

No points

25. Is there a way to provide feedback to improve the overall strategy?

Yes (+4) / No

- **Specific maintenance philosophies**

A methodology for operating the maintenance department

1. Have you adopted any formal work process practices or programs to help your company be more efficient?

Yes / No   No, score this section 0 and move to the next one

2. If so, which ones? E.g. ISO, TQM, TPM…

2 point per program, up to 4 pts

3. At what levels in your company are they implemented?

Company-wide   4
Business area within the company   3
Plant-wide   2
Specific lines in a process, but not all   1

4. How long have they been implemented?

No points

5. How well have they been accepted within your workplace?

No points

6. How much training was conducted to support their implementation?

No points

- **Computer systems**

The computers or CMMS (Computerized Maintenance Management Systems) which help enable the maintenance business.

1. What percentage of your maintenance workforce has basic computer navigation skills?

>95%	4
90-95	3.5
80-89	3
70-79	2.5
60-69	2
50-59	1.5
40-49	1
20-29	.5

2. Have they been trained in all software tasks necessary for their job and can complete them with at least 95% proficiency?

Yes (+4) / No

3. How many hours a week does each maintenance role previously identified spend on a computer? Performing what tasks?

4.

RoleHours a week   Task

No points

Sharing information

5. Is data shared between maintenance and other areas of your business on common systems?

Yes (+2) / No

6. How is it shared?

A. Paper   0

B. Electronically, on a disk   .5

C. Electronically, on the same network   1

D. Electronically, within the same system/software package   2

7. If any are on the same software system, please describe the software packages and how they link the areas of your business?

No points

AIT Devices

8. Are there AIT devices in place at the plant to enable the maintenance business processes?

Yes (+3) / No

9. List the business processes which use AIT devices, how they are used, and what type of devices

No points

9. Are the AIT devices linked to the CMMS?

Yes (+4) / No

10. If so, how are the linked?

Real-time   4

Semi-realtime (hot sync anytime)   2.5

Sync once a day   1

Scoring Spreadsheet Information

The pages that follow are to be used for scoring. The point values are determined by the answers provided for the questions and can be entered into the spread sheet to determine a final score for that section. Each section of a chapter has an average score and the average score for the sections in a chapter determine the score for that chapter.

Just as in school, scoring is based on a 4.0 scale. To assign a letter grade to the score, use the following key:

A+	3.8 or higher
A	3.6 – 3.79
A-	3.4 – 3.59
B+	3.1 – 3.39
B	2.8 – 3.09
B-	2.6 – 2.79
C+	2.4 – 2.59
C	2.2 – 2.39
C-	2.0 - 2.19
D+	1.7 – 1.99
D	1.3 – 1.69
D-	1.0 – 1.29
F	less than 1.0

In order to be classified Class A in a section or chapter, a score of 3.6 or better must be attained. In order to be certified Class A overall, no chapter can have an average score of less than 3.6

				<u>Score</u>
		Plant equipment and/or location structure		
		1		
		2		
		Combined total		
	3		NA	
	4		NA	
	5		NA	
	6		NA	
	7		NA	
	8			
	9			
	10		NA	
	11			
	12		NA	
	13			
	14		NA	
	15		NA	
		16		
		17		
		18		
		Combined total		
		Total for the section - (of 6)		
		Average for the section		
		Bills of Material (BOMs)		
	1		NA	
	2	List examples here	NA	
	3		NA	
	4		NA	
		5		
		6		
		7		
		Combined total		
		8		
		9		
		10	NA	
		11		
		Combined total		

		12		
		13	NA	
		14	NA	
		Combined total		
		15		
		16		
		17		
		18		
		19		
		Combined total		
		20		
		21		
		22		
		Combined total		
	23			
		Total for the section - (of 6)		
		Average for the section		
		Pre-planned maintenance tasks		
		1		
		2		
		Combined total		
	3			
		4		
		5		
		Combined total		
	6			
	7		NA	
	8		NA	
	9		NA	
	10			
	11			
	12		NA	
	13		NA	
		14		
		15		
		Combined total		
	16			
		17		
		18		
		19	NA	
		20	NA	
		21		
		Combined total		
		Total for the section - (of 8)		
		Average for the section		
		Work centers		

		1		
		2		
		3		
		4		
		Combined total		
	5			
	6		NA	
		7		
		8		
		9		
		10		
		Combined total		
		Total for the section - (of 3)		
		Average for the section		
		Authorization documents		
	1		NA	
	2	List answers here	NA	
		3		
		4		
		Combined total		
	5			
	6		NA	
	7			
		8		
		9		NA	
		10		
		Combined total		
	11			
	12			
	13		NA	
		Total for the section - (of 6)		
		Average for the section		
		Special skills		
		1		
		2	NA	

		3	NA	
		4		
		5	NA	
		6		
		7		
		8	NA	
		Combined total		
		9		
		10	NA	
		11		
		Combined total		
		Total for the section - (of 2)		
		Average for the section		
		Change management process		
	1			
	2		NA	
	3			
		4	NA	
		5		
		6		
		7		
		Combined total		
		8		
		9		
		10	NA	
		Combined total		
	11		NA	
	12			
	13			
	14		NA	
	15		NA	
	16		NA	
	17		NA	
	18			
	19		NA	
	20			
		21		
		22		
		23		
		Combined total		
	24			
	25			

		Total for the section - (of 11)		
		Average for the section		

				Score
		Planning, scheduling, and capacity utilization		
	1		NA	
	2	Provide answers here	NA	
	3			
	4			
	5			
	6			
	7			
	8			
	9		NA	
	10			
	11			
	12			
	13			
	14			
	15			
	16			
	17		NA	
	18			
		19		
		20		
		21		
		22		

		Combined total		
		23		
		24		
		25		
		Combined total		
	26			
	27			
	28			
		29		
		30		
		31		
		Combined total		
	32			
		33		
		34		
		35		
		Combined total		
	36			
	37			
	38			
		39		
		40		
		Combined total		
		41		
		42		
		43		
		Combined total		
	44			
	45			
		46		
		47		
		48		
		49		
		50		
		Combined total		
		51		
		52		
		Combined total		
	53			
	54		NA	
		55		
		56		
		Combined total		
		57		
		58		
		Combined total		
	59		NA	
	60			

	61			
	62			
	63			
		64		
		65		
		Combined total		
	66		NA	
	67		NA	
	68			
	69		NA	
	70		NA	
		71		
		72		
		Combined total		
		73		
		74		
		Combined total		
	75		NA	
	76		NA	
	77		NA	
	78			
	79		NA	
	80			
	81			
	82			
	83			
		Total for the section - (of 48)		
		Average for the section		
		Priority systems		
	1			
	2		NA	
	3	Write examples here	NA	
	4		NA	
	5			
	6			
	7			
	8			
	9		NA	
	10		NA	

	11			
	12			
	13			
		Total for the section - (of 8)		
		Average for the section		
		Performing the work		
	1		NA	
	2			
	3			
	4		NA	
	5			
	6			
	7			
	8			
	9		NA	
	10			
	11			
		12		
		13		
		Combined total		
	14			
	15			
	16			
	17			
	18			
	19			
	20			
	21			
	22			
	23			
	24			
	25			
	26			
	27			
	28			
	29		NA	
		Total for the section - (of 24)		
		Average for the section		
		Reporting		
		List answers here		

	2		NA	
	3			
	4			
	5			
	6		NA	
	7		NA	
	8			
	9		NA	
		Total for the section - (of 6)		
		Average for the section		

				Score
		Preventative (PM)		
		1		
		2		
		3		
		Combined totals		
	4			
	5			
		6		
		7		
		Combined totals		
	8			
	9			
	10			
		Total for the section - (of 7)		
		Average for the section		
		Autonomous (AM)		
		1		
		2		
		3		
		Combined totals		
	4			
	5			
		6		

		7		
		Combined totals		
	8			
	9			
	10			
		Total for the section - (of 7)		
		Average for the section		
		Reactive and condition-based (RM & CBM)		
		1		
		2		
		3		
		Combined totals		
	4			
	5			
		6		
		7		
		Combined totals		
	8			
	9			
	10			
		Total for the section - (of 7)		
		Average for the section		
		Backlogs		
	1			
	2		NA	
	2		NA	
	4			
	5		NA	
	6		NA	
	7			
		Total for the section - (of 3)		
		Average for the section		

				Score
		Output of planning systems and ability to meet needs		
	1			
	2			
	3			

	4		NA	
	5			
	6			
	7		NA	
	8	0 days		
		1-3 days		
		3-5 days		
		5-10 days		
		10-20 days		
		20-30 days		
		>30 days		
	9			
	10			
	11			
	12			
	13		NA	
	14		NA	
	15			
	16		NA	
	17			
	18		NA	
	19			
	20		NA	
	21			
	22		NA	
	23		NA	
	24			
	25		NA	
	26			
	27		NA	
	28		NA	
	29		NA	
	30			
	31			
		Total for the section - (of 18)		
		Average for the section		
		Supplier involvement		
	1			
	2			
	3			
	4		NA	
	5			
	6		NA	
	7			
		Total for the section - (of 5)		
		Average for the section		

		Stock usage, safety stock, leverage purchasing		
	1			
	2	Provide answer here	NA	
	3			
	4			
	5			
	6			
	7			
	8		NA	
	9			
	10			
	11	Provide answer here	NA	
		0-3 days		
		3-7 days		
		7-14 days		
		14-30 days		
		30 or more		
	12			
	13			
	14			
	15			
	16			
	17		NA	
	18			
	19		NA	
	20			
	21		NA	
	22		NA	
	23		NA	
	24		NA	
	25		NA	
	26			
	27			
	28			
	29			
	30	Provide answer here	NA	

	31			
	32			
	33			
	34		NA	
	35			
	36			
	37			
	38			
	39			
	40		NA	
		Total for the section - (of 27)		
		Average for the section		
		Parts inventory process		
	1		NA	
	2			
	3			
	4			
	5			
	6			
	7			
	8		NA	
	9			
		10		
		11		
		Combined total		
		12		
		13		
		Combined total		
		14		
		15		
		Combined total		
	16		NA	
		Total for the section - (of 10)		
		Average for the section		
		Parts delivery process (to work area)		
	1			
	2		NA	
		3		
		4		
		5		
		6		
		Combined total		
	7		NA	
	8			

		Total for the section - (of 3)		
		Average for the section		

				Score
		Success measures		
	1	Provide answers here	NA	
	2		NA	
	3			
	4			
	5			
		Total for the section - (of 3)		
		Average for the section		
		Data analysis & continuous improvement		
	1			
	2		NA	
	3			
	4		NA	

165

5				
6				
7				
8				
9				
10				
11				
12				
	13			
	14			
	Combined total			
	Total for the section - (of 11)			
	Average for the section			

				Score
	Organizational structure			
1			NA	
2				
3				
4			NA	
5			NA	
6				
7	Provide answers on worksheet -		NA	
8				
9				
10			NA	
11				
12				
13			NA	
14				
15				
16			NA	
17				
18			NA	
19				
20				
21				
22				
23				

	24		NA	
	25			
		Total for the section - (of 16)		
		Average for the section		
		Specific maintenance philosophies		
	1			
	2			
	3			
	4		NA	
	5		NA	
	6		NA	
		Total for the section - (of 3)		
		Average for the section		
		Computer systems		
	1			
	2			
	3	Provide answers here	NA	
		4		
		5		
		Combined totals		
	6			
	7			
	8	Provide answers here	NA	
	9			
	10			
		Total for the section - (of 7)		
		Average for the section		

		Average scores
Plant data structure		
Plant equipment and/or location structure		
Bills of Material (BOMs)		
Pre-planned maintenance tasks		
Work centers		
Authorization documents		
Special skills		

Change management process		
Total		
Maintenance planning		
Planning, scheduling, and capacity utilization		
Priority systems		
Performing the work		
Reporting		
Total		
Maintenance programs		
Preventative (PM)		
Autonomous (AM)		
Reactive and condition-based (RM & CBM)		
Backlogs		
Total		
Material planning		
Output of planning systems and ability to meet needs		
Supplier involvement		
Stock usage, safety stock, leverage purchasing		
Parts inventory process		
Parts delivery process (to work area)		
Total		
Measures		
Success Measures		
Data analysis & continuous improvement		
Total		
Organizational effectiveness		
Organizational structure		
Specific maintenance philosophies		
Computer systems		
Total		

Maintenance Database

Plant equipment and/or location structure

How to improve:

Every plant has line or process drawings and some information in a file or computer system which identifies the items which make up the process. This is the best place to start. The machinery structure should map to the way the facility is set up, and every part of the plant should be able to use the same structure. In addition, it should represent a hierarchy of processes and sub-processes within a plant.

Other considerations include:

- How much maintenance history is required/desired in your business? To what levels of detail in the line or process is the history required?

- Do you plan to create maintenance Bills of Material (BOMs)? If so, will they be attached to the structure? At what levels in the hierarchy?

- Do you plan to track specific moveable pieces of equipment within the structure? If so, at what levels will they be attached to the structure? Will you track their movement within the structure?

- Do you want to use the structure to identify the location of the maintenance work? If so, what level of detail within the structure of the line do you want to plan the work?

With answers to the above questions, you can get started on building a hierarchy for your plant and company. The decisions made here will have far-reaching impacts on the data structure of your plant and its machinery as well as define the basis of the analysis capabilities of your business. Be sure to understand them before proceeding with the rollout of the structure.

Bills of Material (BOMs)

How to improve:

There are two types of Bills of Material (BOMs) which can be established independently of one another. They are:

1. Object-specific BOMs – These are linked to an object or location within a plant and list the specific items which make up the object. In addition, they can include references to drawings, schematics, digital photos, etc.

2. Maintenance BOMs – The list of parts required to complete a maintenance task.

Potential sources of information to create either type of BOM include:

- line/process drawings
- maintenance cards and manuals
- schematics

With Bills of Material, you can generate a standard parts list for the plant and eliminate unused items, thereby reducing inventories. Also, they can lead to leveraged purchasing based on planning of maintenance material needs from standardized parts lists in planned jobs.

Some considerations for creating Bills of Materials include:

- How much material history is required in your business? To what levels of detail?
- Will the BOMs be attached to a structure? If so, at what levels?
- What kind of material usage history is required in your maintenance work?

With answers to the above questions, you are ready to document your BOMs, attach them to a data structure within your company, and start saving money using standard material lists.

Pre-planned maintenance tasks

<u>How to improve:</u>

Every plant has an existing maintenance program in some form or another. It can be found in computer systems, notebooks, card files, spreadsheets, and your technicians' experience.

The first step is to review the data sources to determine the size and depth of your maintenance program. As you review the information and look for areas of improvement, some questions to ask are:

- Do you have any maintenance programs such as TPM in place?
- How would you classify the pre-planned maintenance task you have in place? Are they Preventative? Autonomous? Predictive/Condition-based?
- How much confidence do you have in your current maintenance program? Is it a list of several items you regularly do or a list of tasks that are performed as necessary? Would you be ready to roll out all or at least a majority of its requirements, automatically?
- Do you have regularly recurring maintenance, which you wish to do in a standard manner but do not want to plan?
- Is it documented in pre-planned tasks as well?
- Are the pre-planned tasks detailed enough for planning purposes?
- Are they detailed enough for a technician to perform the work from?

The establishment of a good pre-planned maintenance program can go a long way towards improving the efficiency of your maintenance business. In addition, it will standardize work processes and maintenance requirements not just for a plant, but an entire company. This standard approach to maintenance work can lead to significant savings in parts and allows for several more opportunities for continuous improvement through benchmarking and other forms of data analysis across all lines and plants.

Work centers

How to improve:

The data within work centers can be as detailed or simple as you desire. They can be created to represent an organizational hierarchy within your plant and to capacity plan the time of a specific maintenance individual.

Some considerations for establishing work centers are:

- Will the capacity of the work center be planned? If so, to what level - for the entire work center or for each individual?
- Will any special skills of the work center or individual be noted and used regularly for reference by a planner?
- Will the people in the work center be budgeted? If so, how often and to what level of detail?

The answers to these questions will help you establish a work center hierarchy to better capacity plan and budget the time of your maintenance team. From there, capacity and cost planning can be viewed across departments and an entire plant. This will assist in the planner with the allocation of resources to meet as many maintenance needs as possible within the labor cost restrictions.

Authorization documents

How to improve:

Work authorization can be as finite and detailed a process as necessary to meet safety and quality considerations.

These documents could be required for the following reasons:

1. Approval for a maintenance task to begin
2. Certain special skilled or supervisory personnel to be present to witness a maintenance event
3. To record completion of the task
4. Any required quality certification.

When creating an authorization process, the following steps are recommended:

- Identify the work where authorization requirements exist
- Identify who or what level person has to sign off the work
- Determine the type of authorization required – before, during, or after the work
- Where is the authorization documented
- Conduct an audit of how often this process is currently used correctly
- Identify why the process was not followed in cases where steps were skipped

Every maintenance business has some kind of work authorization process for any variety of reasons. It is essential this process is well documented and adhered to. Following these steps should get a maintenance business started towards a strong authorization and documentation program which should meet the needs of any internal or external inspectors as well as protect the safety of your personnel.

Special skills

How to improve:

Using standard special skills, which are identified in a standard manner, can be very useful for detailed maintenance planning and assist with work completion. Some tips for getting it started include:

- In order to identify the special skills that are recognized within the company there are three usual sources of information:
  1. Review the human resource records of the company to see if there are already accepted skill sets in place
  2. Review the maintenance tasks for special skills and skill levels
  3. Review the maintenance certification that pertains to your type of work

- From the tabulated list, review the records of personnel to identify the skills they have and their levels of expertise and document them in a place the planners can use (E.g. HR records, work center records, or planning spreadsheets). (Skill examples: expertise, skill – basic welder, advanced pipefitter, expert electrician).

- Utilize the information in work planning for personnel assignments, capacity planning, and work completion

Following these steps should get a maintenance business started towards a well-organized and finitely planned work force which will improve its overall efficiency and productivity.

Change management process

Maintaining the data accuracy of maintenance records in whatever format to reflect the current structure and to record production, maintenance, performance, and cost history.

How to improve:

Once a database has been established, data change management will be a constantly ongoing task for a plant. After the data is collected, whether in spreadsheets or a computer, someone will need to make sure its integrity is maintained by keeping it current and accurate.

The first consideration is who will own this task and at what levels will data be controlled in an organization. One factor in this decision will be the amount of standardization required within a business. If you would like to do detailed comparisons as part of a continuous improvement program, a fairly high level of standardization is recommended. In that case, the person in this role will need to have significant technical ability and the authority to make and/or work through data decisions. This could include changing standard work processes in pre-planned work tasks, creating or deleting master data records, and defining and ensuring the entry of data for line/process improvements.

The examples of possible database changes are too numerous to mention. But they fall into three basic categories. They are:

Routine in-plant changes	Equipment movements, configuration changes resulting from maintenance events, and other changes which may occur during the normal operation and maintenance of the business.
Project-related changes	When large scale projects alter plant configuration
User-requested changes	User recommendations for improvements of plant equipment or processes of to fix inaccuracies in the database

In any case, an administrative structure and process must be in place to support the data integrity requirements necessary to run the business. Additionally, it must help maintain the accuracy of the data collected so it is current when at start-up.

Depending on the complexity of the company, a high level of standardization is recommended and, possibly a few full-time positions for the people who manage the creation and changing of your database. A software package can provide a database to help better mange your maintenance business. The work processes you implemented to support the software will outline how you choose to use it within your business. If you plan to mine that database for continuous improvement you will find data integrity to be very important.

Finally, as part of the process, a database change request procedure will be needed. There are several options for routing these requests. They include e-mail systems, company forms, or within the maintenance database system. The last option is recommended, as it keeps all maintenance data in one system, but it depends on the organization and computer hierarchies of the company.

Maintenance Programs

Preventative (PM)

How to improve:

Every business has its own planned maintenance program. It is some combination of preventative and autonomous maintenance activities which are performed to keep the machinery or processes at their optimal operating condition. The tasks may be a product of supplier recommendations, items learned and added while performing PMs, and a technician's experience. When improving a PM program, first assess the reliability of the execution and follow-up documentation. Then determine the amount of change/upgrade to be performed to the program. Once complete, the new tasks are integrated into the existing planned maintenance program. Within a few months, you can start the continuous improvement program and review the database for trends and learning in order to make future improvements.

Autonomous (AM)

How to improve:

The goals of every Autonomous Maintenance program are identified as:

- Prevent equipment deterioration through correct operation and daily checks
- Bring equipment to its ideal state through restoration and proper management
- Establish the basic conditions needed to keep equipment well-maintained

In order to meet these goals, the following steps are recommended:

- Identify the autonomous maintenance tasks
- Determine responsibility
- Train the employees and supervisors
- Develop a plan for the work
- Execute & document
- Improve through focused improvement

These steps outline how to improve or get started on an autonomous maintenance.

Reactive and condition-based (RM & CBM)

<u>How to improve:</u>

Every company has reactive maintenance in one form or another. However it is documented, it must be integrated into the overall maintenance schedule and then completed. Regardless, many of these tasks may be able to follow the same procedures each time, e.g. start up and shut down procedures, post-fire inspections, line changeovers. A planner can create pre-planned tasks which are not scheduled, then use them as templates to generate orders in a much faster and standardized manner. Using these pre-planned reactive maintenance tasks, planners could reserve the necessary resources and cost the work, then integrate them into the existing maintenance schedule. Then they are resolved and documented. Then, a continuous improvement program could review them and potentially turn them into planned maintenance. Reactive maintenance usually covers 70-80% of work performed by maintenance personnel on a daily basis. A program which documents, plans, and completes these tasks in a consistent and efficient manner will be very beneficial to any company in terms of cost savings and can lead to focused improvement efforts which will reduce the overall amount of reactive maintenance.

Backlogs

How to improve:

While documenting the backlog of maintenance work, one of the best ways to manage the tasks is to integrate them into the existing pre-planned maintenance schedule, which essentially eliminates the need for a backlog. A planner could schedule them into existing time slots and then complete them on a specific date, instead of as time permits. Thus there is no list of jobs waiting to be completed, every one has a planned completion date with resources assigned, etc. Not only will this help with resource and capacity planning, but will help you prioritize what jobs are to be done when or if they need to be completed at all. This is the best long-term strategy for a maintenance department, eliminating the backlog and turning everything into pre-planned work will greatly increase the efficiencies of the maintenance department as well as all the supporting organizations.

Maintenance Planning

Planning, scheduling, and capacity utilization

How to improve:

Author's note: The time span and amount of detail you can put into your short and long range planning is practically boundless. You may want to think about an environment where all AM and PM work is rigidly planned with no backlog of reactive work. My experience comes from an environment, where the goal was 95% of all maintenance work was to be planned 30 days in advance. The other 5% (reactive work) was planned as well, working it into the already existing downtime blocks. Every job had a time and date where it was scheduled for completion. It was performed at that time unless unplanned downtime occurred and the job could be moved forward, thereby decreasing future planned downtime needs. I mention this to stretch your mind about the possibilities of your PM program. The savings opportunities are <u>very</u> substantial by integrating this kind of planning with your production schedule and PM material needs. With this in mind, the following information details how to establish a finite maintenance planning program for your company.

To get started, maintenance mangers will need to review and analyze their maintenance historical data. That includes the maintenance schedule (plan vs. actual completion), MTTR, MTBF, resource lead times, downtime, PMs, etc.

From there, the maintenance department can get a better understanding of their department and start to communicate with the other areas of the plant their needs.

It is in the pre-planning that a maintenance department can best understand their requirements and communicate them to the production planners in order to get a completely integrated manufacturing schedule for both department which they can truly live with. With the above information as a guideline, any company can refine their own program to improve their planning systems and take them to levels of productivity rarely seen in manufacturing today. For an example, see Appendix C.

Priority systems

How to improve:

There are two types of priority systems, object-specific and task-specific.

1. Object-specific – Object-specific priorities are assigned to equipments and line/processes within a plant. They can be based on a program which looks at things like safety, process bottlenecks, production requirements, costs, and effects on other processes. A value is "calculated" and assigned to the reference object. This "ranking" can be updated regularly based on changing business needs, process changes, etc and can be set up to be viewed in each work order.

2. Task-specific priorities identify the importance of the task being reported and planned. The priority levels give pre-established levels of importance to a task. Additionally, they can provide pre-determined scheduling parameters for more accurate planning and resource allocation.

Some companies choose to use both types of priority systems, especially when capacity planning for an entire site. Object-specific priorities give the planner a "site-wide" perspective of the business needs, while the task specific priority allows them to balance it with the importance of each job. By using the two, they would have truly objective resource planning, based on data.

Notes:

Preventative maintenance tasks (PMs) should not have a priority. Each company should have a PM program they are committed to and perform as planned. Not only will it keep up machine productivity but if PMs are not preformed regularly, you will be unable to get consistent data to know what items are worth doing and which should be deleted.

Performing the work (and follow-up documentation)

How to improve:

Obviously, the accurate and timely performance of the maintenance work is the most important part of any maintenance program. However, some of the items in the process below may be able to help your program

1. Once an order is created, labor, materials, and resources may be collected and charged to the work.

2. The skilled technician gathers the required materials and documentation for the maintenance task and verifies their correctness (Ideally they are delivered to a pre-established maintenance staging location near the job.) Additionally, they verify all resources are available, including the time and any special skils or services. If there are any shortfalls, the technician resolves them with the planner prior to commencing the work.

3. Next, the technican performs the work correctly and on time.

4. Once maintenance is complete, the skilled technician must complete their part of the follow-up documentation. This work could include entering any actual data required in the shop papers making suggestions for improvements, and identifying any additional work discovered.

Author's Note: The infamous quote "the job is not done until the paperwork is finished" could not be more applicable. In order to get many of the advantages a CMMS provides, you must complete the follow-up documentation for each work item. It is imperative you stay on top of this data workload and complete in a timely manner. Otherwise, you will not be able to keep the system current and all attempts to mine the database for improvements will be incomplete.

Reporting

<u>How to improve:</u>

Because of the diversity of each business, it would not be practical to list the specific reports of every line of business. However, there are two areas almost every type of company can look at to improve:

1. Report paralysis – If the report does not meet one of the three previously listed reasons for reporting, then it is not necessary. Also, look to combine reports where many data fields are similar. A well thought-out report reporting program usually needs approximately 30 percent of those currently in place.

2. CMMS and online reporting – Once a report is generated on paper it is out of date. Paperless reporting with real-time data can help management make the best business decisions.

To track system performance and implement improvements the maintenance leadership should have a series of pre-established reports. They would provide the data necessary for comparison and benchmarking. With this information, the maintenance leaders can recommend planning and maintenance system improvements for their business operations, thereby improving reliability and saving money.

Budgeting

How to improve:

Budgeting for maintenance work centers has gone on for many years. With the ever-changing requirements of the work force, it is important all facets of their job are accounted for. Thus, ensure the following are included in the budget

A. The total costs for the following items for the personnel in your work center:
- Travel
- Training
- Wages
- Benefits
- Vacations
- Consumables
- Meetings
- Overtime

B. Based on previous performance, estimate a percentage of production time lost due to unplanned downtime and the requirement of maintenance personnel to make the repairs.

C. Planned maintenance hours for production and the requirement of maintenance personnel to perform the planned maintenance.

These numbers should be provided to the accounting personnel who determine an hourly rate for the maintenance folks to bill internally.

From there, a planner can track their annual actual budgets against the plan. Mistakes in budgeting is one of the fastest ways to get in trouble as a maintenance manager. Thus, many of the planning mechanisms earlier mentioned can help you determine a more accurate budget plans and actuals. The proof is usually in the numbers and the more accurate and detailed the numbers the clearer the picture, hopefully for the better.

Material Planning

Output of planning systems and ability to meet needs

<u>How to improve:</u>

Planning material needs can be a quick way to start showing maintenance savings. Some useful techniques include:

- Implementation of an Material Requirements Planning (MRP) strategy to best manage the material request, identify their priorities and timelines, and meet the material needs accordingly

- Sharing material requirements across business areas can lead to lower inventories and purchase prices due to leveraged buying

- Material firm zones are established to uphold purchasing lead times and help with scheduling

- Prepare the items for each order in the storeroom, and deliver them ready for use at line three to five days before the work is to be done

Following these steps should get a maintenance business started towards a well-organized and finitely planned work force.

Supplier involvement

How to improve:

Involving the supplier in the inventory determination process can enable a much smoother and more cost effective supply chain. Some useful techniques include:

- Share planning data between supplier and company to help the supplier get the parts to the company just-in-time, so it doesn't sit in the inventory of either party.

- Having known and set lead times will minimize expediting of parts while maximizing planning and savings

- Leveraged purchasing leads to significant savings for both supplier and user

- Supplier maintains safety stock the customer for long lead items and some critical items in the supplier's inventory. Sometimes the supplier charges a fee to hold the materials, but it should be cheaper than the cost of the customer maintaining the inventory themselves.

These ideas can help build a much improved supply process and lead to significant savings for both supplier and customer.

Stock usage, safety stock, leveraged purchasing

How to improve:

Ineffective processing of material requests can cause material costs to grow rapidly. Some useful improvement techniques include:

- Establish one parts request process that is integrated with all purchase requests within the plant, preferably within a computer system. Such a system helps with documentation, cost accounting, allows for the easy and accurate transfer of data between departments, and helps identify turnover rates for parts. Regardless, one standard purchasing process for all items maximizes purchasing efficiencies and savings.

- Improve parts management in the storeroom by using:
  - Pre-staging (kitting) parts for maintenance work by work order number
  - Material requirements planning to plan the procurement of maintenance materials
  - Priority systems within the storeroom to fill kits in the correct order and resolve material need conflicts
  - Establishing and upholding firm planning zones for materials to minimize expediting

- Review actual usage data to set safety stock levels and leverage purchasing, removing any parts no longer used in the plant

These concepts can enable the processes of a storeroom become much more efficient and accurate.

Parts inventory process

How to improve:

Ineffective inventory management can cause material costs to grow rapidly. Some useful techniques to improve include:

- One standard, company-wide numbering system with complete and up-to-date master records which contain usage, technical specification, purchasing, and planning information.
- Make inventory records available in easy to access database, integrated within the plan.
- Continuously audit inventory and master record data accuracy with a goal of at least 98% correct.
- Information for maintenance materials within each plant will be contained in the Bill of Materials for each piece of equipment. The storeroom will stock materials based on the Bill of Materials. Inventory levels will be set by planed maintenance. There may be exceptions based upon long lead time and criticality, but all stocked parts should be in a BOM for a piece of equipment used in the plant.
- A clear owner for the daily management of all inventories should be established. This includes managing the items in the inventory as well as maintaining the record accuracy. Inventory usually includes finished products, intermediates, raw materials, spare parts, and packing materials.
- Establish a clear Inventory Record Accuracy process to monitor the accuracy of inventory transactions (item, location, quantity, status, and lot where used) and to focus improvement efforts through root cause analysis. It should be maintained at or above 98 percent to ensure effectiveness of production scheduling, material planning, and procurement activities.

These items will lead to a very accurate and well-managed inventory which will better identify and serve the material needs of the facility as well as provide for significant savings through a more efficient process.

Parts delivery process (to work area)

<u>How to improve:</u>

A parts delivery process, which requires all maintenance parts to be ordered through work orders, can significantly improve the productivity of the storeroom and maintenance personnel. For the maintenance personnel, it will keep them from spending time in the storeroom browsing for the parts, which will give them more time to complete work and maximize uptime. For the storeroom personnel, it will allow them to concentrate on filling more orders and have fewer distractions or less traffic in the storeroom. Some techniques for implementing a delivery procedure include:

- Establish a regular parts delivery process where storeroom personnel bring complete work kits to the maintenance site. Also, include in this program a regular location and time for maintenance personnel verify parts and sign for them.
- Deliver the parts for a each job 3-5 days prior to the scheduled date of the task. Thus, when unplanned downtime occurs, a maintenance person can immediately pull work forward which is planned for an upcoming downtime period and complete it while performing the critical repair. This maximizes the unplanned downtime and reduces future planned downtime.
- All maintenance materials will be processed via a centralized storeroom which can be accessed by qualified individuals only. The storerooms will stock to safety stock levels only. All other parts will be purchased when needed and delivered to the work site or nearest staging area three to five working days before the job is planned to be done.

These ideas can lead to tremendous time savings for storeroom, maintenance, and even production personnel. Thus, the company can increase worker productivity and product by reducing downtime.

Measures

Success Measures

<u>How to improve:</u>

Most companies have a set of success criteria in place to monitor their business. However, the following steps are recommended to review the validity of that criteria and possibly add new measures.

1. Identify the long and short-term business goals – for the company, plant, and line/process levels
2. How are they measured? How often? What equation is the score assigned?
3. Verify that the measures are documented and train the people how to achieve them
4. Evaluate their success and improve the measures as necessary.

Following these steps will help you focus the business on its most important goals through clearly identified and standardized measures. Focusing on your measures and how to achieve them correctly should lead to short-term improvements and continued long-term success.

Data analysis & continuous improvement

How to improve:

One of the best reasons to buy a CMMS should have been data analysis for continuous improvement. If you do not have a formal CMMS, many of your calculations will be more difficult. However, at a minimum, you should be able to review location and equipment history including PM and production performance, labor and material usage and costs, and planned vs. actual data. Also, one can perform comparisons across similar locations and equipment in the same or different business areas to look for areas of improvement.

A CMMS offers a great deal of data analysis possibilities for continuous improvement. To begin such a program, the following steps are recommended:

- Determine the primary areas of improvement
- Determine responsibility for the program and its execution
- Execute the program, implement improvements, and look for new opportunities to improve

The ultimate goal of a continuous improvement program is to move as much maintenance into a predictive preventative maintenance program which narrows the component replacement curve and maximizes productivity while driving down unnecessary inventories.

Organizational Effectiveness

Organizational structure

How to improve:

The organizational structure of a company can have a very significant effect on the efficiency of the work force. In addition, how that structure is implemented and carried out on a day-to-day basis must be known amongst all employees at all levels. In order to ensure these goals are met, the following items are recommended:

- The roles of each employee should be in writing and include their responsibilities, who they report to, etc
- Each person should be trained in what is required in their role and what the company goals are
- A rewards and evaluation system should be in place and known

Once every employee knows what is required of them, the managers of the company can spend the bulk of their time managing the parameters their people work within and meeting the changing needs of their business. That is what defines a truly progressive and productive company, one in which everyone knows their role and can use that knowledge to look to the future.

Specific maintenance philosophies

How to improve:

When choosing from the several maintenance philosophies available today, two of the most important questions to ask are:

- What they do for you?
- How well can it be carried out in the work place?

It is the opinion and experience of the author to recommend TPM as the best one available today. Although it was not the intention, using TPM and an integrated computer system is what will enable a business to reach the highest marks in this evaluation program. The best recommendation is to select a philosophy which works best in your line of business and stick to it.

Computer systems

How to improve:

Regardless of the CMMS a company has chosen, there are three key concepts which determine their effectiveness. They are:

- Training – Every operator must receive training in the required tasks they are to carry out within the system. In addition, some form of documentation, paper or electronic, should be available for them to easily refer to when performing these tasks.

- Usage standards – There must be "buy in" at all levels to use the CMMS when called for to enable the work processes. This means no purchasing parts outside the system, no extra work performed without documentation, etc. In addition, users must adhere to the data standards for completing the records in the CMMS. They must complete each required field the correct information. Without either of these sources of information, a continuous improvement program can not be as effective and accurate as possible and may results in less than the best possible decisions for the business.

- Integration – The more integrated the CMMS, the better it is able to enable all the work processes in your company because everyone is working from the same set of data. This point cannot be stressed enough.

Selecting the right CMMS and developing the best enabling work processes will make across the board improvements and significant savings for your company. If you do not have one, and one that is integrated, I strongly encourage you to look into making a change as soon as possible.

Making the Business Case for Maintenance

It has been my experience that the only thing that is lower in the totem pole than maintenance is training. When it comes times to make business decisions, sales and production are always the driving factors, sometimes regardless of the impacts and potential costs incurred down the road because of cutting back on maintenance.

Generally speaking, part of the reason maintenance is not considered in these decisions is that management looks at the near term impact on the bottom line, not the long-term impact, and often have bonus and/or promotion goals attached to meeting their numbers this year, leaving future problems to future management.

However, I also think that maintenance personnel have some responsibility for this as well. Many maintenance managers can draw upon their experiences when reciting the impacts of pushing out or canceling maintenance on production machines. However, often their warnings of future problems are received as 'crying wolf' and are usually discarded. It is very important that maintenance managers can come to these meetings with data that shows the impact of decisions made and what will happen in the future.

The production managers bring business case analyses to these meetings and the plant mangers make go-no go decisions. Maintenance managers need to get their data and put it in a similar business case format.

A CMMS will help the maintenance manager get the data and help format it using the same approach as a production manager. By showing the plant manager how this improvement will eliminate these problems that are costing the company $n and have a return on your investment in n months, the decisions might be more likely to be integrated instead of driven by production.

Example business case document:

(Not every improvement/issue would need a totally completed form like the one above, but the more data which can be presented to the plant manager, the more solid your point is made and the more likely it will be heard

The last 4 pages are supporting documentation which can be borrowed from when making the business case.)

Business Case Document:

1. SUMMARY

1.1. SUMMARY: (brief outline of business case – typically written after detailed business case has been substantially completed)

2. CURRENT STATE (AS-IS) ASSESSMENT

2.1. CURRENT BUSINESS MODEL / STRATEGY: (brief outline of present state)

Identify issues about operation, technology, competition, customer service, employees, stakeholders, etc

3. FUTURE STATE (TO-BE) ASSESSMENT

3.1. BUSINESS SOLUTION: (outline of future business solution)

3.1.1. More specific description of new process (step-by-step with details and possibly a flowchart)

3.2. GAP ANALYSIS : (identify gaps between as-is and to be solution)

Process	Gap	Options	Recommendation

3.3. APPLICATION TO FACILTIES/SITES:

3.3.1. FACILITIES/SITES IN-SCOPE: (identify all locations in-scope)

3.3.2. FACILITIES/SITES OUT OF SCOPE: (identify all locations not in scope)

3.4. IDENTIFY LEGACY & OTHER SYSTEMS AND PROCESSES:

3.4.1. SYSTEMS/PROCESSES TO BE ELIMINATED: (identify current systems to be replaced)

3.4.2. SYSTEMS/PROCESSES TO BE INTERFACED: (identify current or new systems to be interfaced)

3.4.3. SYSTEMS/PROCESSES TO BE IMPLEMENTEDSTAND ALONE: (identify current or new independent systems)

3.5. HANDLING HISTORICAL DATA/PROCESSES: (identify how present and past data will be dealt with)

3.6. ON-GOING SUPPORT REQUIREMENTS: (identify personnel and physical resources)

3.7. CONTINUOUS IMPROVEMENT OPPORTUNITIES: (identify potential future projects)

4. IMPLEMENTATION PLAN

4.1. IMPLEMENTATION OBJECTIVES: (state reason(s) for implementation project)

4.2. IMPLEMENTATION SCOPE:

    4.2.1. BUSINESS SOLUTION IMPLEMENTATION: (identify business solution to be implemented)

    4.2.2. ORGANIZATIONAL ALIGNMENT: (identify change management requirements)

4.3. IMPLEMENTATION PROJECT TEAM:

    4.3.1. IMPLEMENTATION PROJECT TEAM COMPOSITION: (identify team members & skills)

    4.3.2. IMPLEMENTATION PROJECT TEAM SCHEDULING: (identify numbers required over time)

4.4. IMPLEMENTATION PROJECT TRAINING:

    4.4.1. PROJECT TEAM TRAINING: (identify training requirements for team members)

    4.4.2. EXECUTIVE TRAINING: (identify training requirements for senior management/executives)

    4.4.3. MANAGER/SUPERVISOR TRAINING: (identify training requirements for mid-level executives)

    4.4.4. END-USER TRAINING: (identify training requirements for staff/users/workers)

    4.4.5. FOLLOW-UP TRAINING: (identify training requirements following implementation)

4.5. IMPLEMENTATION PROJECT TIMELINE: (graphic high-level implementation plan)

4.6. IMPLEMENTATION PROJECT MEASURES: (identify measures to be used for implementation)

5. CRITICAL PROJECT ASSUMPTIONS ASSESSMENT:

5.1. ASSUMPTION ANALYSIS: (identify key assumptions and comment on each below)

Assumption	Analysis/Comments
1.	
2.	
3.	
4.	

6. RISK/OPPORTUNITY ASSESSMENT:

6.1. RISK ANALYSIS: (identify risks; for each, assess probability of occurring, level of importance, action which could prevent the risk, and action which could be taken to deal with it if it should occur)

Risk ➢ **P = Probability** *(H-M-L)* ➢ **I = Impact** *(H-M-L)*	P	I	Preventive Action (Action to prevent risk from occurring)	Contingency Action (Action to be taken if risk occurs)
1.				
2.				
3.				
4.				

6.2. OPPORTUNITY ANALYSIS: (identify opportunities; for each, assess probability of occurring, level of importance, action which could help ensure the opportunity is realized, and action which could be taken to deal with it if it should not arise)

Opportunity ➢ **P = Probability** *(H-M-L)* ➢ **I = Impact** (H-M-L)	P	I	Promotive Action (Action to encourage development of opportunity)	Contingency Action (Action to be taken if opportunity does not occur)
1.				
2.				
3.				
4.				

7. COST/BENEFIT ANALYSIS:

7.1. COSTS:

7.1.1. IMPLEMENTATION (ONE-TIME) COSTS: (quantify initial & other one-time costs)

7.1.2. RECURRING COSTS: (quantify on-going costs, preferably on net present value basis)

7.2. BENEFITS: (identify quantifiable and qualitative savings here and, in detail, below)

    7.2.1. OPERATIONAL SAVINGS:

    7.2.2. CYCLE TIME IMPROVEMENT SAVINGS:

    7.2.3. QUALITY IMPROVEMENT SAVINGS:

    7.2.4. WORK VOLUME/EFFICIENCY SAVINGS:

    7.2.5. REVENUE INCREASES:

    7.2.6. MARKET SHARE/COMPETITIVE POSITION IMPROVEMENTS:

    7.2.7. IMPROVEMENTS FOR CUSTOMERS:

    7.2.8. IMPROVEMENTS FOR EMPLOYEES:

    7.2.9. RETURN ON INVESTMENT ESTIMATES:

8. RECOMMENDATIONS:

8.1. RECOMMENDATIONS: (list recommendations to senior management)

8.2. CONCLUSION: (state appropriate closing remarks)

9. APPENDIX:

9.1. LIST OF DOCUMENTS (list and attach all desired detailed documents such as detailed descriptions of each business solution function/module, implementation plan charts, cost charts and tables, and other detailed documentation that might provide useful background information to senior management)

An Integrated PM Program
Helps Achieve Two Goals
Which Will Lead to Significant
Business Savings

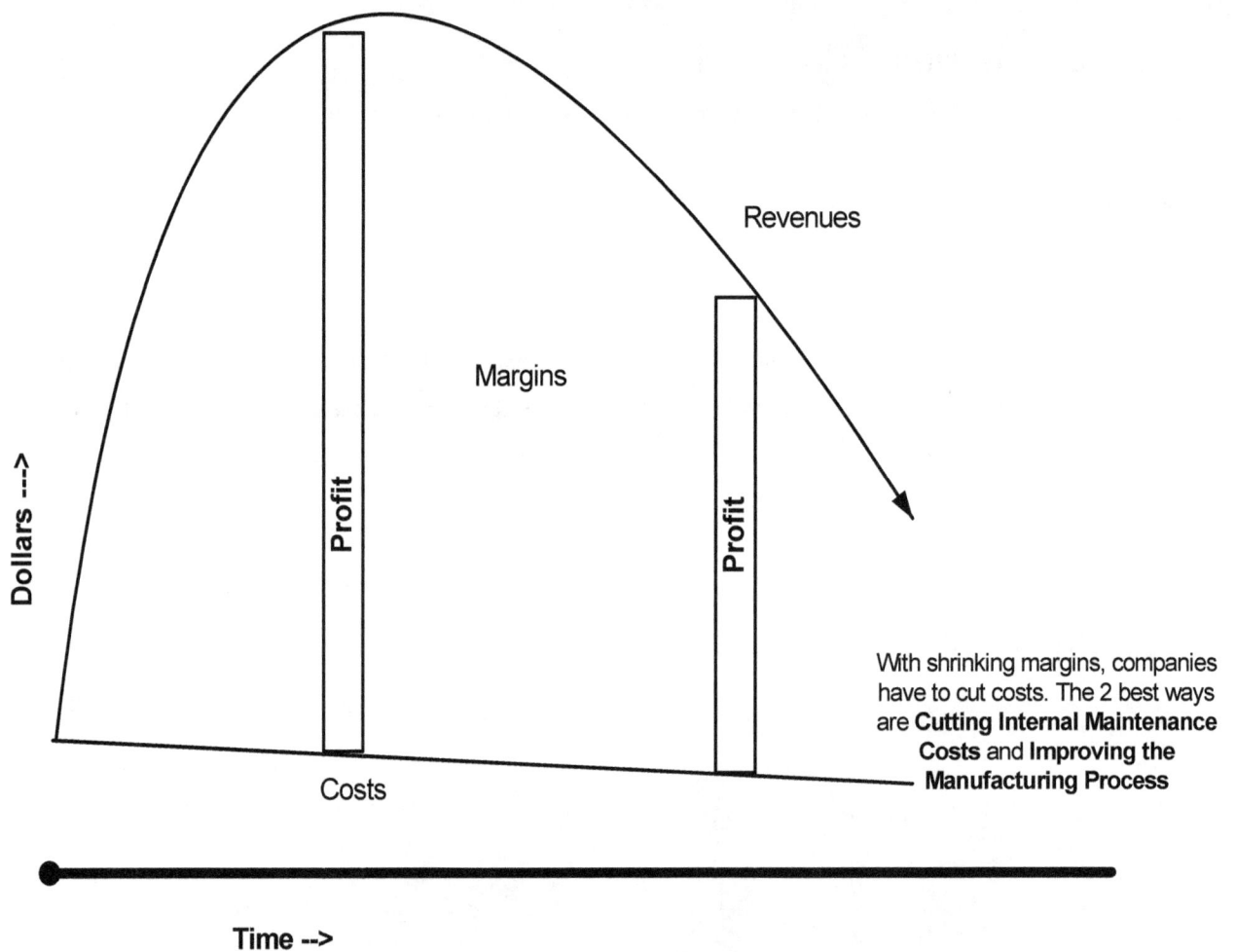

Revenues

Margins

Dollars --->

Profit

Profit

With shrinking margins, companies
have to cut costs. The 2 best ways
are **Cutting Internal Maintenance
Costs** and **Improving the
Manufacturing Process**

Costs

Time -->

Cutting Internal Maintenance Costs
and
Improving the Manufacturing Process

BENEFITS OF AN INTEGRATED PM PROGRAM

Improved Manufacturing Process

- ➢ Gain the ability to improve manufacturing up-time
- ➢ Increase asset life through improved preventive maintenance
- ➢ Improve ability to troubleshoot through analyses of similar objects affected, and previous problem descriptions and causes
- ➢ Justify asset overhaul or replacement through detailed work history and cost analyses
- ➢ Identify maintenance opportunities to improve performance through:

    Identification of problem and cost trends

    Benchmark comparisons

    Statistical analyses of mean time between repairs, mean time to repairs
- ➢ Implementation of coding system to better classify maintenance problems, their causes, and the activities to repair them
- ➢ Capture counter and performance readings for equipment for maintenance history and planning purposes
- ➢ Two objective maintenance prioritization systems, one for the event, the other for the choke points in the factory
- ➢ Generate an aggressive autonomous and preventative maintenance program based on maintenance history data
- ➢ Completely integrated production and maintenance plan where maintenance downtime can be planned at the S&OP level
- ➢ Enable comprehensive lock-out/tag-out program
- ➢ Quality checks, measuring points, and counter readings can be recorded and reviewed for continuous improvement
- ➢ Enable all maintenance and improvement programs such as TPM (Total Productive Maintenance) 6 Sigma, and Class A.

Cut Internal Maintenance Costs

- ➢ Identify opportunities for optimizing maintenance performance
- ➢ Justify expenditures for predictive maintenance technologies
- ➢ Optimize spare parts inventory to minimize inventory costs (purchase, stocking, taxes, *etc.*)
- ➢ Bring "maverick inventories" under control through reliable ATP checking
- ➢ Optimize maintenance resource utilization through improved capacity planning

➢ Standardized, easy-to-use reporting which report costs instantly up the hierarchy

➢ Reduce inventory of unused/obsolete parts and lowering safety stock levels by using MRP with material lead times and reviewing material turn-over rates

➢ Reliably track maintenance activities performed for non-maintenance purposes (capital and expense projects, *etc.*)

➢ Identify future maintenance resource needs such as temporary staffing for holidays, outages, etc

➢ Bring one of the largest of corporate expenditures under tighter control

➢ Define where parts are used

➢ One data source for all maintenance information

➢ Automatically generate a purchase request and link to the order needing the service or part

➢ Reduce overtime through better planning

➢ Develop a standardized, objective work prioritization system

➢ Maintain a hierarchy of all plant equipment with serialization history

➢ Auto-enable response profile for maintenance technicians based on a priority system

➢ Standardized work processes for preventative and reactive maintenance

➢ Web-enable some or all of data and functions to the technicians and internal customers

➢ Standardized business processes across all maintenance areas, leveraging improvements and geometrically increasing savings across the plant or multiple plants

➢ Dispatching of resources using a variety of methods and send/link to specific problem information

➢ Certifications and qualifications of maintenance personnel, along with their individual availability can be tracked and maintained

GOAL: To totally change the maintenance rewards system – Your best preventative maintenance "Maytag repairman" should always be more recognized than your best Corrective maintenance "Firefighter."

POSSIBLE PERFORMANCE METRICS

PRODUCTIVITY

- Production uptime
- Mean time to be repaired
- Mean time between failure
- Top 10 product problems (scrap)
- Top 10 most expensive repairs
- Top 10 problem areas (product line location, etc)
- Technical history based on: Performance readings and counters, Problem and Resolution codes, etc
- Parts usage history

COSTS

- Annual maintenance cost (dollar amount)
- Annual maintenance cost as percentage of other corporate expenditures:
  - Overall annual expenditures
  - Annual capital plan
  - Annual marketing budget
  - *etc.*
- Annual maintenance materials (spares) costs (dollar amount)
- Annual materials (spares) cost as percentage of:
  - Total materials purchases
  - Raw materials purchases
  - Finished goods
  - *etc.*
- Approximate total inventory count for maintenance spares
- Annual savings if spares inventory could be reduced by:
  - One percent
  - Five percent
  - Ten percent
  - *etc.*
- Estimate of amount of "maverick" inventories currently in place
- Annual savings attributable to these potential uptime increases
- Preventative maintenance costs, effectiveness
- Reactive maintenance costs, effectiveness

SERVICE

- ➢ Service response time
- ➢ Repair time in repair center, by part, by job
- ➢ Tracking repair part through the repair center
- ➢ Tracking service event throughout process
- ➢ Maintenance scheduling effectiveness

Appendix: Example Policies

This appendix is a collections of policies and measures to give you some ideas to help implement the maintenance improvements you have found through your audit. Feel free to use them as necessary to support your new processes.

Maintenance Database

- There must be an owner assigned with the responsibility of creating and maintaining the technical database. The responsibilities of the owner include:

  - Developing the change management systems that will be used.

  - Define the data to be stored in the maintenance database and at what levels will it be managed.

  - Entered the information into the database and start to maintain its accuracy

- All parts, equipment, and their locations will be documented in accordance with company data standards to support integration, benchmarking, and rapid continuous improvement of business results

- Standardization begins with the design of improvement projects from engineering and continues throughout the maintenance processes. All projects must have as a deliverable updating the technical database to reflect the changes which occur as a result of the scope of the project.

- Consistent BOMs within all plants, particularly in terms of format and data.

- A complete equipment BOM which lists spare parts, non-store items, and other equipment, is necessary to ensure parts are available and allocated for planned maintenance.

- One overall maintenance database within a site which shares information electronically with other areas of the plant

- The TDB is accurate and up-to-date at all times relative status of the equipment and their locations.

Maintenance Planning

- Maintenance planning will be a continuous, 18-month process concurrent with the other long-range planning processes within the company. All maintenance planning will be tied to the master production schedule (MPS), where planned maintenance downtime is part of the overall planning process which includes accomplishing all technical requirements

- Pre-determined production downtime windows will be used to facilitate planned maintenance.

- Firm zones will be 21 days in advance for maintenance and production planning to stabilize advanced planning. The only changes to be made in the overall production/maintenance schedule in the final seven days before any maintenance task are those caused by a breakdown or safety event.

- 95% of all completed maintenance orders will be planned and integrated into the master production/maintenance schedule 21 days in advance.
- An objective ranking process will assist planners with the prioritization of work and resource allocation.
- ALL maintenance work will be in the form of a work order or notification
- ALL routine reactive maintenance work shall be initially reported in a notification. This includes routine reactive maintenance from condition monitoring or operation of equipment, any kind of improvement projects, or other type of work required from maintenance personnel. They will be written to the lowest possible level within the maintenance structure and can be completed by any plant personnel.
- In the event of an emergency, a notification may be bypassed and a work order written to obtain the necessary resources to resolve the problem. This work process streamlines the resource acquisition process and provides for rapid repair of the breakdown. However, once the repair is made, a notification will be required as follow-up documentation to record the event and for future data analysis.
- Improvements use data based on accurate information for decision making. Improvements are aimed at total business improvement to gain budgetary leverage, for example, better planned maintenance reduces storeroom inventories.

Material Planning

- All maintenance materials for a plant are managed through a central storeroom.
- Material planning treats storeroom and purchasing as one system that provides parts based on planned work.
- A vendor-managed material supply system that directly sends the part from the vendor to the person that wrote the work order is established.
- Material planning provides early notification to purchasing/stores operations so materials inventories can be managed to a lower inventory level at a lower unit cost. Material requests come from planned maintenance work orders. Materials do not require expediting.
- Maintenance must supply the storeroom with the specifications for materials. These specifications should be based on standardized materials and assemblies. The standardization must be based upon operational data. The storeroom is responsible for ensuring that materials stocked meet these specifications.
- All maintenance materials will be processed via a centralized storeroom which can be be accessed by qualified individuals only. The storerooms will stock to safety stock levels only. All other parts will be

purchased when needed and delivered to the work site or nearest staging area three to five working days before the job is planned to be done.

- All spare parts in the storeroom will be linked to a current BOM.
- One standard for a materials pick-up and delivery system will be in place.
- All maintenance materials for a plant will be issued from and returned to the Central Storeroom. Credits may be applied based on storeroom procedures.

Measures and reports

- Percent maintenance database complete
- Number of database errors detected (in a weekly audit of 20 records)
- Percent of database changes made within 24 hours of their change made on the operating floor
- Percent of overall work process followed
- Percent of fields accurately completed
- Percent of problems reported correctly
- Percent of problems corrected in the appropriate time frame
- Precent of problems planned correctly
- Percent of labor time entry performed correctly (including follow-up documentation)
- Percent of orders which were reactive
- Percent of orders which were emergency reactive
- Percent of parts which were delivered on-time to the maintenance area.
- Percent of orders filled correct to the parts request in the order
- Number of out of stock situations
- Percent of parts delivered to the storeroom correctly from external sources
- Percent of maintenance personnel trained to use the CMMS
- Percent of maintenance personnel qualified to use the CMMS
- Number of database changes submitted
- Percent of changes made to the database within 24 hours of being submitted
- Percent of work orders completed per the daily work schedule
- Percent of work orders completed per the 21 day work schedule
- Overall line productivity
- Total downtime (daily)
- Total process stops (daily)
- Total downtime due to unplanned maintenance (daily)

- Maintenance and repair spending (costs/unit produced)
- Parts usage history
- Work order cost history
- Breakdown analysis
- MTTR/MTBF
- Damage analysis
- Remove no longer useful maintenance tasks
- Location analysis
- Exception analysis
- Changing PMs to AMs and vice versa
- Equipment structure list
- Improving maintenance tasks
- Cost analysis
- Plan vs. actual costing of maintenance plans

Life Cycle Tracking in the Army

Introduction:

The goal of this white paper is to summarize the Life Cycle Tracking (LCT) efforts currently in the Army and propose a solution for LCT in SAP.

Discussion:

Life Cycle Tracking (LCT) is monitoring a serialized item throughout its entire existence in a company. That means from Acquisition to Scrap. It is important each aspect of the item's life cycle work together to give a complete picture of the serialized item. This coordination means complete and consistent data collection which can enable continuous improvement efforts like root cause analysis. Item tracking and data analysis are the keys to the success of any LCT program, especially as it tries to improve readiness and control costs. It is the reason most companies look at LCT, to help them "do more with less."

Often, projections on item problems and expected repair workload are primarily made from mortality data (i.e., "We broke 50, so we need to have 50 fixed for next year when we will break 50 again."). A complete LCT program looks deeper into the problem by allowing users to ask questions such as, "Why did 50 of those items break?" "What are the contributing factors (geography, users, what specific s/n installed at, usage (hi/low), etc) of those breakdowns?" This root cause analysis (a finite breakdown of item problems and their reasons why) will significantly reduce overall maintenance costs while improving operational readiness. The primary enabler of this root cause analysis, as found in the Total Productive Maintenance (TPM) methodology, is life-cycle serial number tracking. This method of tracking allows users to bar code the serial numbers on the items and sub-assemblies and establish item hierarchies with parent-child relationships. Thus, data collection and root-cause analysis can be preformed at level of the item hierarchy.

Root cause analysis is a very powerful maintenance analysis tool and provides the following advantages for a maintenance business:

- Solving maintenance problems by research and analysis (brain) not volume of resources (brawn)
- Decreasing failures and downtime
- Lower costs because inventory requirements are lower (less failures)
- More accurately predict failure rates
- Provide for better provisioning data

- Enables predictive maintenance – replace before failure, eliminates unplanned downtime and gets to maintenance repair pipeline faster

In any working environment with mature business processes, the savings that can be realized through maintenance improvements are usually geometrically greater than any other business process improvement. The areas above are prepared to start down the path towards LCT and the savings and readiness improvements they can bring. However, it is important to identify all of the opportunities where LCT can bring improvements.

Just as importantly, it is essential the correct level of LCT is implemented. Over implementation of LCT can lead to suffocation of the day-to-day business process. While under implementation will lead to lower levels of savings and readiness improvements.

Thus there are some key requirements, which must be taken into consideration before a LCT program is implemented. They are:

- Common data system with common data standards – one has to ensure all data efforts support each other and that their requirements do not inhibit a complete LCT solution.

- Data collection – Each aspect of business will need to vigilantly collect data to the same level and update the system real-time. A CMMS can smoothly enable this requirement and give all users real-time visibility of an item's performance. Thus, enabling root cause analysis at any point of the item's life cycle. This will provide for better troubleshooting with a stronger, a more accurate troubleshooting database and enable item improvement initiatives at all levels of engineering and design.

- Serial number tracking will be required to levels lower than the top end item. An effort must be undertaken, by item, to determine the necessary level of serialization. At a minimum, cost of serialized item, reliability (of item), and mission criticality should be taken into consideration. In addition, configuration management must be vigilantly maintained in a common database. From a data analysis point of view, it does not matter where (depot, field) or why (problem, re-man, cannibalization) something is removed from an item, but it does matter when and how something was removed and what replaced it. The choices made around serialization and configuration management in this step will go a long way in determining how successful a LCT program will be.

Additional advantages of a LCT program include:

- Warranty tracking which can be performed at any serialized level and rolled up or down to superior or subordinate items.
- Capturing and tracking performance readings for a serialized item
- A common place for electronic storage of data by serialized item, which eliminates the need for log books which travel with the item
- Allows all locations visibility of items users are to work on before they arrive, which would significantly help their planning and resource gathering (*including critical long lead-time parts*) for the repair of these items thus reducing set-up costs and repair cycle time.

The goal of every LCT program is threefold. Firstly, significant cost savings would be realized in several areas due to less failures, lower inventories, and shorter repair cycle time. Secondly, the reliability of the item would be increased, thus improving readiness. Finally, better knowledge of the item would improve troubleshooting techniques and making repairs and improvements faster.

In order to meet these goals and realize the savings a Class A data Plant Data structure should be created including the requirements outlines above.

Appendix C:

MCPP

- Maintenance
- Continuous
- Planning
- Process

An 18-month, finitely detailed, continuously updated, maintenance plan, which includes all known maintenance work and the required resources.

Overview

The purpose of the Maintenance Continuous Planning Process (MCPP) is to ensure maintenance activities and associated material capacity are clearly defined and agreed upon in order to meet production and maintenance requirements. Maintenance materials planning assures zero lost equipment downtime and/or human effort hours due to maintenance part(s) availability. The MCPP is developed to organize and resolve maintenance activity and material planning issues for the next eighteen months. The plan collects and prioritizes pending and projected work and ultimately balances machinery needs against budgetary requirements.

Process Relationships

The Maintenance Continuous Planning Process (MCPP) takes the information from the Technical Database and puts the recurring preventative maintenance items into motion. It provides a detailed picture for maintenance leadership to interface with other business areas (D&S - Integrated Planning and the S&OP Process, Purchasing - material needs for maintenance work, Production - downtime inputs to the production schedule, and Accounting - costs for maintenance work) as well as within each piece of the maintenance business. It also provides data for completion of autonomous maintenance performed by line operators.

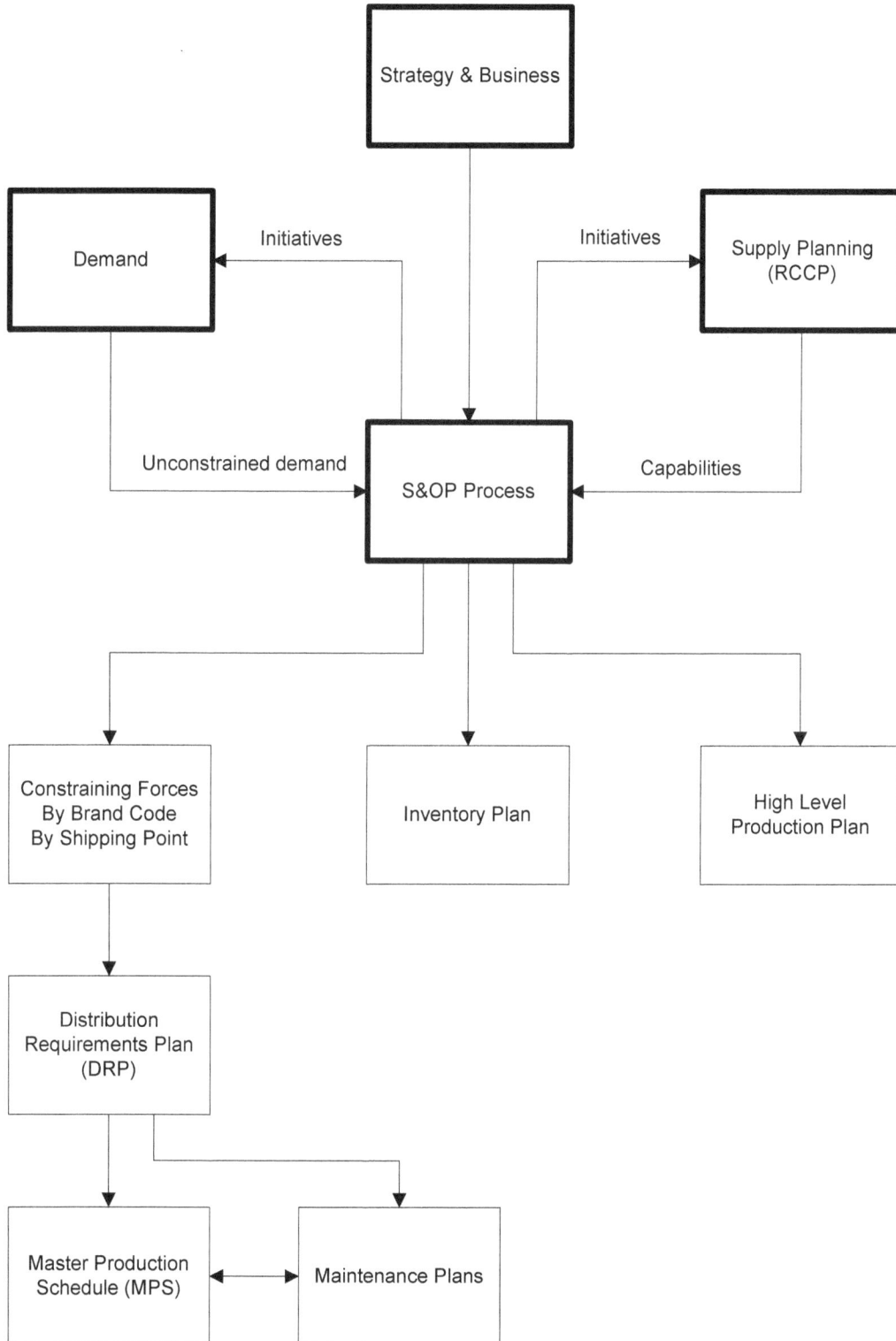

S&OP Process

```
                    ┌─────────────────────┐
                    │  Strategy & Business │
                    └─────────────────────┘
                               │
                               ▼
┌──────────────┐  Initiatives        Initiatives  ┌──────────────────┐
│    Demand    │◄───────────┐   ┌──────────────►│  Supply Planning  │
│              │            │   │                │      (RCCP)       │
└──────────────┘            │   │                └──────────────────┘
        │                   │   │                        │
        │ Unconstrained     ▼   │                        │
        │   demand      ┌──────────────┐   Capabilities  │
        └─────────────►│ S&OP Process  │◄────────────────┘
                        └──────────────┘
                          │    │    │
        ┌─────────────────┘    │    └──────────────────┐
        ▼                      ▼                        ▼
┌──────────────────┐  ┌──────────────┐      ┌──────────────────┐
│ Constraining     │  │ Inventory    │      │   High Level     │
│ Forces By Brand  │  │   Plan       │      │ Production Plan  │
│ Code By Shipping │  │              │      │                  │
│ Point            │  └──────────────┘      └──────────────────┘
└──────────────────┘
        │
        ▼
┌──────────────────┐
│  Distribution    │
│ Requirements Plan│
│     (DRP)        │
└──────────────────┘
        │        └────────────┐
        ▼                     ▼
┌──────────────────┐  ┌──────────────────┐
│ Master Production│◄►│ Maintenance Plans│
│  Schedule (MPS)  │  │                  │
└──────────────────┘  └──────────────────┘
```

S&OP Process

The Sales & Operation Planning (S&OP) process is an integral part of an overall business strategy. This monthly review is conducted at the general manager level with the goal of developing an overall 18-month plan for all facets of their business.

Maintenance has input at the highest part of the planning process by providing production constraints to the supply side of this process. They include downtime in monthly buckets by line, by month; planned costs; and resource requirements.

The output of the S&OP Process will be the framework from which the Master Production Schedule (MPS) and the MCPP will be developed and updated.

Maintenance Continuous Planning Process (MCPP)

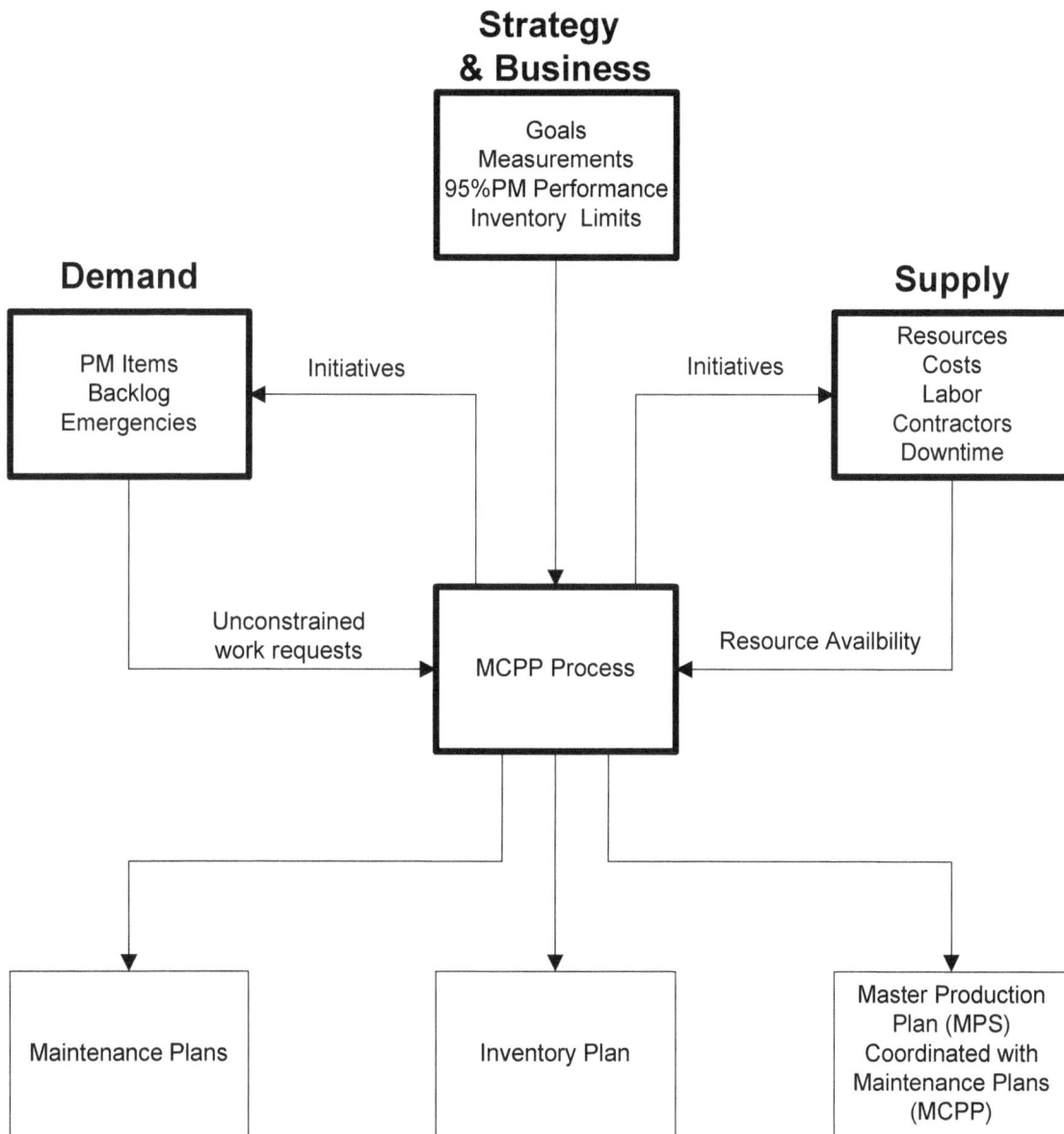

Strategy & Business

Goals
Measurements
95%PM Performance
Inventory Limits

Demand

PM Items
Backlog
Emergencies

Initiatives

Supply

Resources
Costs
Labor
Contractors
Downtime

Initiatives

Unconstrained work requests

MCPP Process

Resource Availbility

Maintenance Plans

Inventory Plan

Master Production Plan (MPS) Coordinated with Maintenance Plans (MCPP)

Maintenance Continuous Planning Process (MCPP)

The MCPP is a continuous planning and review process for all known maintenance work in the next 18 months. It permits no backlog of work as all work will be planned into a pre-established downtime or while-running block of time.

This process is very similar to the S&OP Process but with differing data. In the MCPP, the Strategy & Business goals are measures. They include:

95% Planned maintenance performance 30 days in advance

98% IRA

98% TDB Accuracy

Reliability goals

The Demand is all the possible maintenance work. It can come from many sources and includes all PMs, reactive work and emergency items. The Supply, in MCPP terms, means resources and their availability and capacity for work. They include:

Downtime available

    Contractor availability

    Overtime

    Costs

    Labor capacity to perform work

    Components

The Maintenance Planners and Business Leaders use the MCPP and the functional location rankings to determine their priorities within their work lists; develop their downtime buckets; and plan their work within them, including a critical path for each bucket. The resultant plan provides the following outputs:

    Maintenance work plan

    Inventory plan for Storeroom

    Integrated production and maintenance plan

In order to get started with the MCPP the following is required:

    Data collection

    Data creation in a CMMS

Specific operating parameters and policies

Data collection

A complete Technical Database must be in place before starting the MCPP. This includes all the data outlined in two previous documents which detail the requirements for functional location, equipment, and assembly records, Bills of Materials, and pre-planned maintenance tasks. Once that data is entered, plans can be created and requirements generated to begin your MCPP.

Maintenance Planning

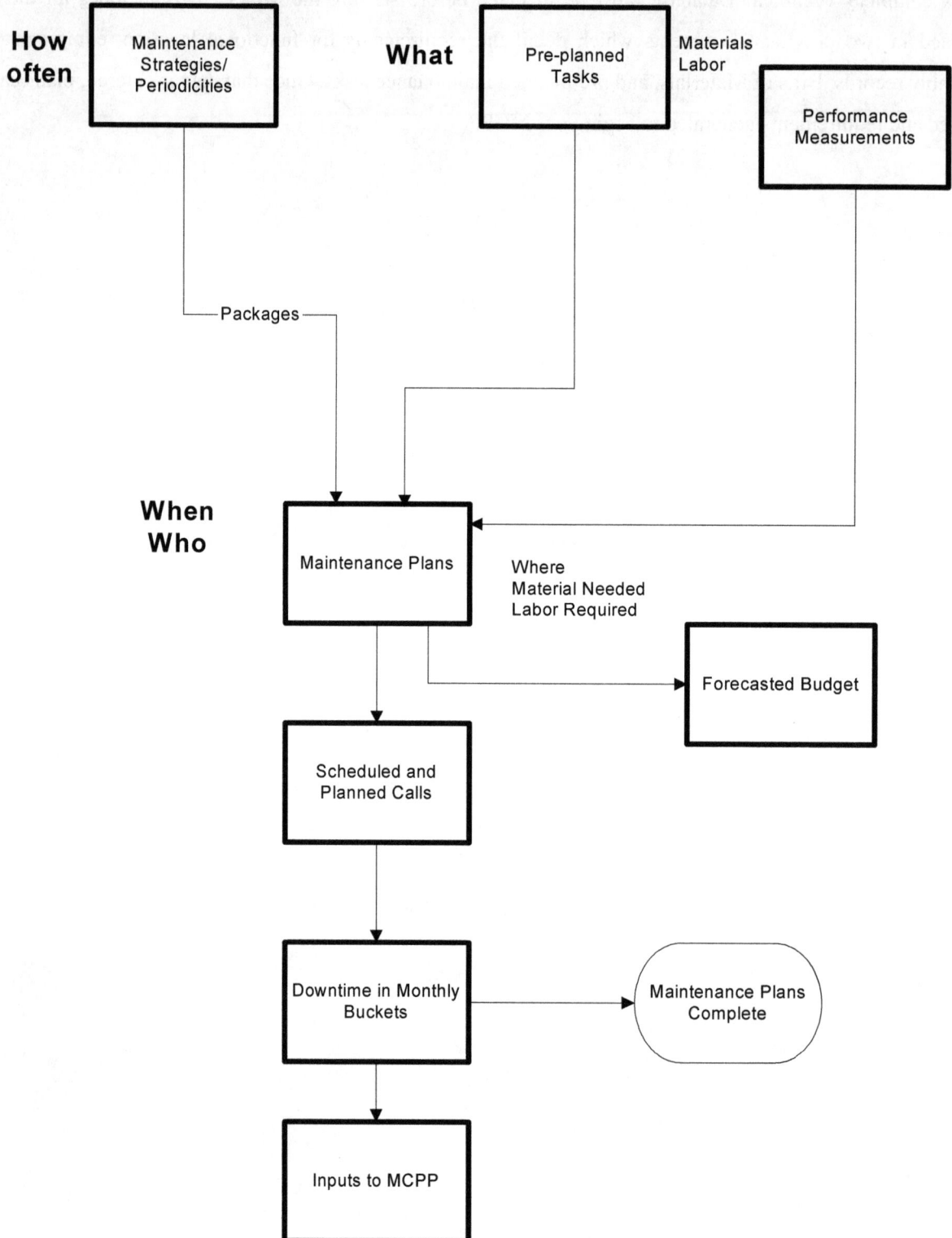

How often — Maintenance Strategies/ Periodicities

What — Pre-planned Tasks — Materials Labor

Performance Measurements

Packages

When Who — Maintenance Plans

Where Material Needed Labor Required

Forecasted Budget

Scheduled and Planned Calls

Downtime in Monthly Buckets → Maintenance Plans Complete

Inputs to MCPP

Data Creation

The preceding chart outlines how data must be created to enable maintenance planning.

Maintenance strategies/Periodicities are the basic periodicities in which you intend to plan work. Maintained at the company level, these are based on specific pre-established units of planning called packages. Each package is a multiple of the unit of planning and is assigned to the operation (maintenance task) you are planning to perform at some frequency. There are two types of strategies. They are:

Time-based - based on the calendar e.g. days, weeks, months…

Performance-based - based on a unit you configure e.g. cycles, gallons, run-hours…

For example, MPWEEK is a weekly strategy with packages 1W (1 week), 2W (2 weeks), 3W, 4W, 6W, etc… Each operation within a task list (pre-planned maintenance task) is assigned to a package based on the frequency you wish to perform this task. That operation will eventually become part of an order created from that task list.

SAP works similarly with performance-based strategies. DICYC, a cycle-based (cycles are a unit of production performance) strategy with a starting unit of 1 million cycles (1MM) has packages of 10MM, 20MM, 30MM, 60MM, 80MM, 120MM, etc.… Each operation will be due the day the CMMS predicts the cycle frequency will be achieved. For example, An operation which starts at 900MM cycles has a periodicity of 60MM cycles. SAP will use an estimate of annual cycles you pre-establish to determine the day the operation will be due (the cycle 960MM is achieved) and create an order to perform the work on that date.

Pre-Planned Maintenance Tasks (task lists) are the basic template for standard work processes for specific maintenance items.

Reactive task lists - If there are maintenance processes for tasks you wish to plan but cannot plan regularly – e.g. firefighting, tag-outs, etc. - you can create a task list and copy it into a work order whenever needed.

Planned task lists - Here is where your PM and AM programs are created. You will plan the resource requirements for each task (operation) and assign a periodicity (package in a strategy) which you plan to complete the work.

Once complete, task lists are linked to maintenance plans in order to create work orders automatically.

Performance Measurements are equipment or location readings and counters that are taken. These documents record production performance and can enable maintenance plans to create work orders. There are two ways to use a measuring point. One is to take readings at the location or equipment they are assigned. E.g. temperature, flow rate, etc. This is to document the operating status at the time the reading was taken. The second is as a counter which records production, flow, run-hours, etc.

Maintenance plans create the PM and AM schedule. They combine the data from the assigned records (strategies, task lists via items, measuring points) and create work orders based on the parameters you establish in the plan.

There are three types of plans. Both time-based and performance-based create work orders from task lists based on these strategies. Only, performance-based plans require a measuring point.

Time/Performance-based plans are a combination of the two. The planner configures the packages to be used within the plan. E.g. 3 months or 10M miles, 6 weeks and 10MM gallons. One can also set up plans to auto-create orders when measuring point readings do not meet the required parameters. E.g. Temperature must be greater than 100 F and less than 212 F or an order is created.

The outputs of maintenance plans are a forecasted budget for all AMs and PMs and the work orders to plan this work. We will be able to look at what orders are coming due in the next 750 days (scheduled calls), however we will only create the work order in SAP 93 days (3 months) in advance. These orders will reserve resources including parts, labor, special tools and equipment. From this data, the planner can start to develop their MCPP.

Policies & Parameters for the MCPP

- Maintenance planning will be a continuous, 18-month process concurrent with the S&OP process.
- Pre-determined production downtime windows will be used to facilitate planned maintenance.
- All maintenance planning will be tied to the master production schedule (MPS) and S&OP process, where planned maintenance downtime is part of the S&OP process to accomplish technical requirements.
- Firm planning zones will be used to stabilize advanced planning. The only changes to be made in the overall production/maintenance schedule in the final seven days before any maintenance task are those caused by an emergency or safety event.
- 95% of all completed maintenance orders will be planned 30 days in advance.

- An objective ranking process will assist planners with the prioritization of work and resource allocation.
- Firm zones will be 30 days in advance for maintenance and production planning.

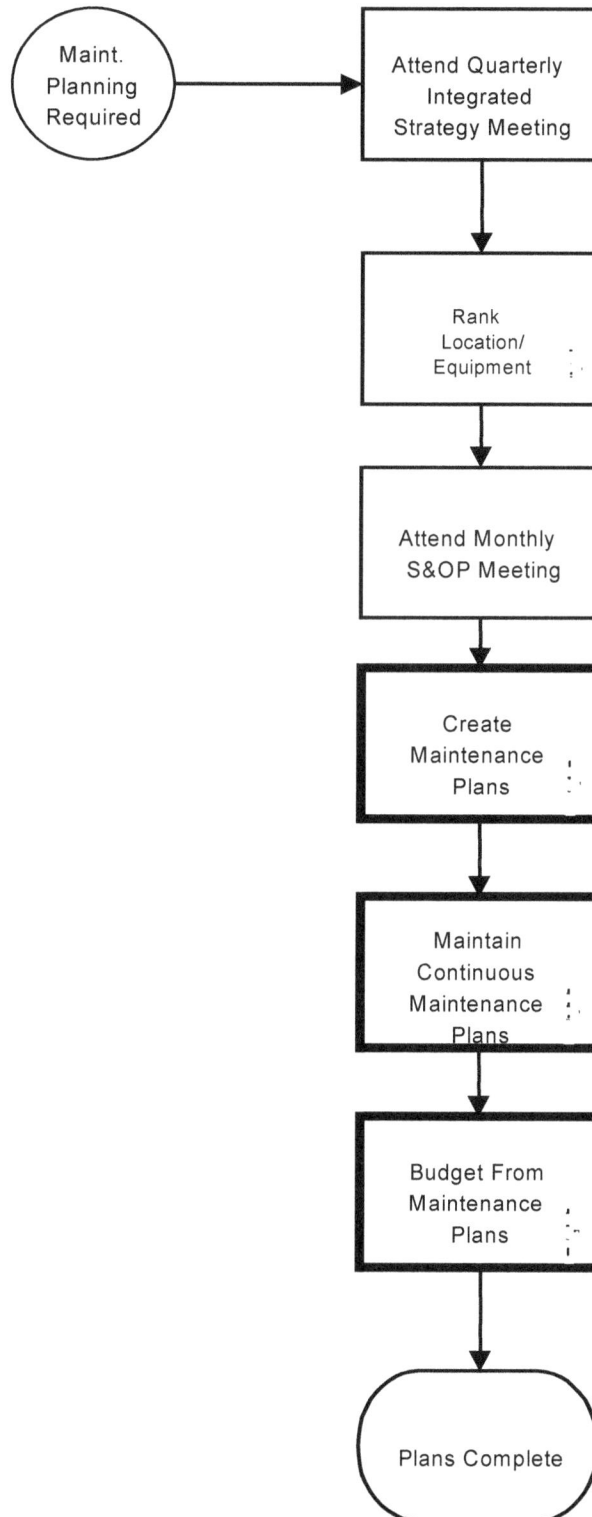

```
┌──────────┐         ┌──────────────────┐
│  Maint.  │         │  Attend Quarterly│
│ Planning │────────>│    Integrated    │
│ Required │         │ Strategy Meeting │
└──────────┘         └──────────────────┘
                              │
                              ▼
                     ┌──────────────────┐
                     │       Rank       │
                     │    Location/     │
                     │    Equipment     │
                     └──────────────────┘
                              │
                              ▼
                     ┌──────────────────┐
                     │  Attend Monthly  │
                     │   S&OP Meeting   │
                     └──────────────────┘
                              │
                              ▼
                     ┌──────────────────┐
                     │      Create      │
                     │   Maintenance    │
                     │      Plans       │
                     └──────────────────┘
                              │
                              ▼
                     ┌──────────────────┐
                     │     Maintain     │
                     │    Continuous    │
                     │   Maintenance    │
                     │      Plans       │
                     └──────────────────┘
                              │
                              ▼
                     ┌──────────────────┐
                     │   Budget From    │
                     │   Maintenance    │
                     │      Plans       │
                     └──────────────────┘
                              │
                              ▼
                     ┌──────────────────┐
                     │  Plans Complete  │
                     └──────────────────┘
```

Maintenance Continuous Planning Process (MCPP)

MCPP provides for:

- Resource Management
- Functional Location Ranking Process
- Continuous Planning Process Integrated with Production
- Autonomous Maintenance System

Resource Management

Resources are defined as:

- Labor

    Skills

    Effort hours

- Materials

    BOMs - material allocations

    Direct link to material planning for storeroom

- Contractors

    Integration with CBS system

    Contractor planning

- Special Tools

    Special "needs" planning

- Costs

    On-demand budgeting

    Cost planning

The MCPP provides the planner the data to know

- who and what you need
- when
- how long

- how many

Equipment/Location Ranking Process

The Equipment/Location Ranking Process is a quarterly review of a site's unit operations by its maintenance leadership. Based on the answers to the following questions a ranking is assigned to each unit operation in the site. The goal is to identify the business need and process bottlenecks and rank them by importance to the overall operability of the site. Based on that data, a planner can make objective decisions on prioritizing work requests and resource allocation when shortages occur.

Item	Factors Evaluated	Rank 1	Rank 2	Rank 3	Rank 4
Points		**3**	**2**	**1**	**0**
Safety	Malfunction's effect on the outside environment?	Failure to complete work violates health and/or safety operating standards	X	X	None
Production	What is the reliability required to meet the production needs?	90% reliability needed	80% reliability needed	65% reliability needed	Less than 50% reliability needed
	Are there other alternatives in case of failure?	No alternatives available	Production can be delayed	Production covered by stock or other	Alternate equipment available
	How does this equipment/ location affect other processes?	Affects the entire plant	Other processes are unable to meet their production requirements	Minimal effect on other processes	No effect
Quality	How does the results of this equipment/ location affect finished product quality?	Product completed undeliverable	Defective finished products greater than 5%	Defective finished products less than 5%	No effect
	What percentage of scrap produced is caused by the equipment/ location?	10% or greater	5 - 10%	2 - 5%	0 - 2%
Reliability	What percentage of maintenance downtime is caused by this equipment/ location?	10% or greater	5 - 10%	2 - 5%	0 - 2%

Maintenance Issues	What is the cost effectiveness of delaying maintenance at this equipment/ location? What percentage of average actual monthly maintenance costs are against this functional location?	Delay will incur costs greater than 10 times cost of the work	Delay will incur costs 5 to 10 times cost of the work	Delay will incur costs less than 5 times cost of the work	No effect
		10% or greater	5 - 10%	2 - 5%	0 - 2%

Equipment/ Location Ranking

A = 27 - 25

B = 24 - 22

C = 21 - 19

D = 18 - 16

E = 15 - 13

F = 12 - 10

G = 9 - 7

H = 6 - 4

I = 3 - 0

For each equipment /location, answer each question above.

Add the point totals for each answer to get the total point value for the equipment/location.

Compare that number against the priority table to determine equipment/location priority.

Letter A is highest priority

This process is to be conducted quarterly by plant.

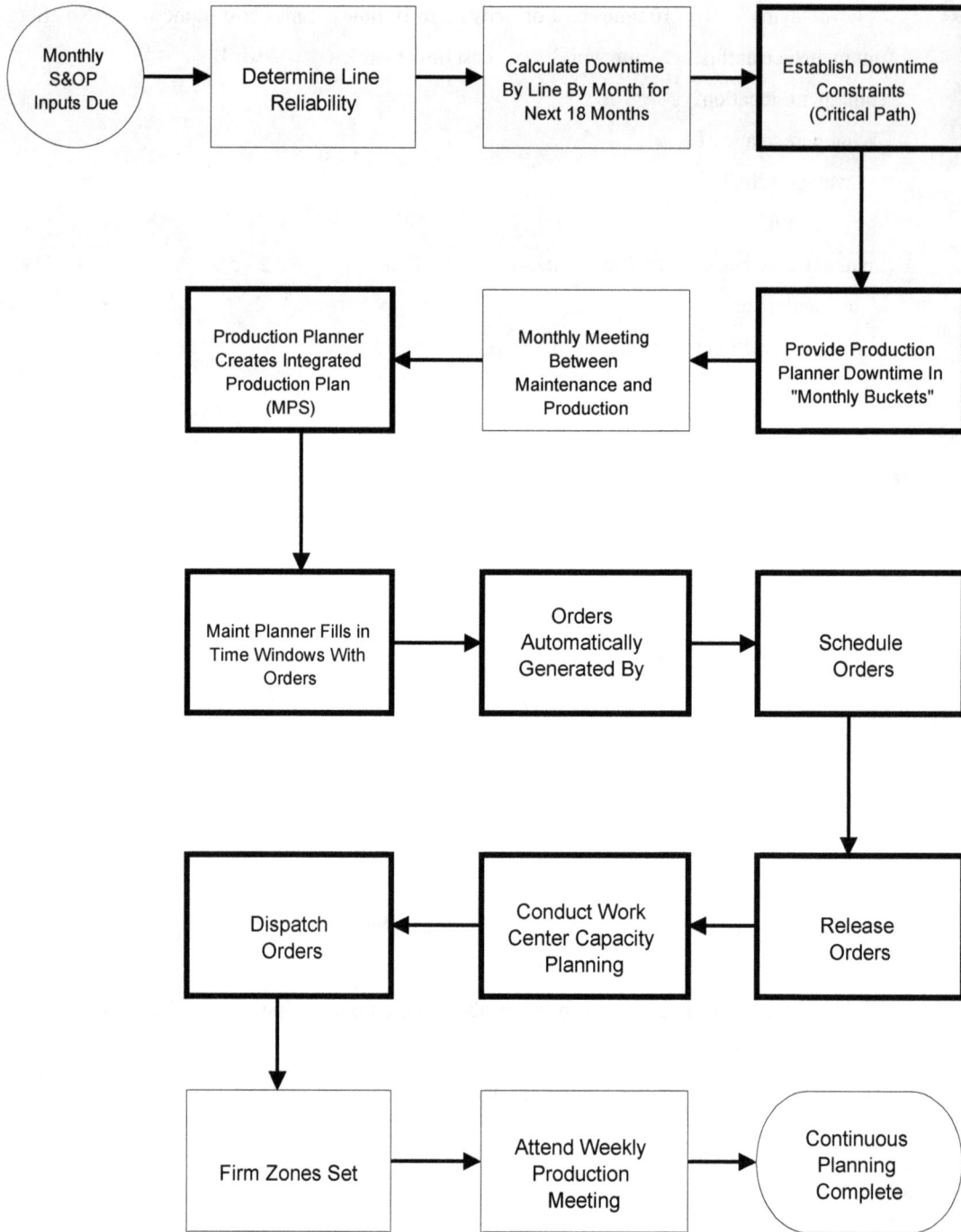

Maintain Continuous Maintenance Plans (MCPP)

Creating the MCPP

Introduction:

The MCPP is an 18-month continuous planning process which is modeled after a company's Sales and Operations Planning (S&OP) process. It obtains the total demand for maintenance work and balances those requests against the total amount of resources (supply) available for maintenance work. Using the functional location ranking process and business goals, the MCPP process prioritizes the work and makes objective decisions for completing all requests for maintenance work.

The MCPP starts with the global reliability number. Reliability is determined based upon previous performance (efficiencies), planned initiatives, changeovers, projected sales, and planned technical requirements. This number will be determined by line by month and will become the basis for downtime for each month.

The maintenance planner uses the number to calculate the downtime requirements, by line, by month with constraints and develops a critical path for maintenance work. Inputs are provided to the production planner in downtime blocks with constraints attached to enable the block to be scheduled to a firm position in the production plan. The production planner will work to build the product schedule around the maintenance constraints.

Once the integrated production/maintenance schedule is complete, the maintenance planner will schedule the work orders into the production intervals (downtime blocks). An objective ranking process will assist planners with the prioritization of work and resource allocation. In the period from 93 to 30 days before the work is due, the planner refines the schedule and resource requests and resolves any issues, including work center capacities.

Firm zones lock-in finite down time windows 30 days in advance. Changes may only be made in the overall production/maintenance schedule, seven to 30 days prior to the maintenance task by agreement with maintenance and production personnel. No changes may be made without concurrence of both PP <u>and</u> PM leadership. No changes are permitted in the final week of the firm zones unless in an emergency or a safety situation exists.

The ultimate goal of the MCPP is to reduce maintenance costs through implementation of a "highly planned" maintenance program and improvement of activity effectiveness and efficiency. In addition, the MCPP provides the link between maintenance order execution, maintenance capacity requirements planning, maintenance material planning, and the master production schedule. The use of firm zones for planning maintenance work is essential to ensure the requirements of the maintenance orders are held true for finite order planning and changes can be made only in emergency situations. This forward-looking method of maintenance scheduling maximizes the ability to conduct material planning which uses specific lead time data to purchase materials on a just-in-time basis in order to reduce inventories and lower unit cost.

The maintenance planner is the central point of contact for each of these tasks within the maintenance organization. They plan and schedule all work and act as the primary interface between maintenance and production personnel. Much of their work is done in the 1-18 month planning window. Once the 30 day firm planning zone is met, the planner turns over a firm schedule to be implemented by a maintenance technical leader or maintenance functional leader.

How it works:

Determine Line Availability:

The Expected Productivity Goal for each line is the start of the process. We will not change how it is calculated, this process uses the number to determine the amount of downtime available for maintenance.

Factors which determine the Expected Productivity Goal include:
Previous Performance
Changeovers
Efficiencies
Projected Sales
Technical Requirements - determined by Maintenance Personnel

Maintenance planners will use the MCPP to determine the technical requirements for each line.

Calculate downtime by month for next 18 months

In this step, planners will use the percentage of technical requirements to determine the number of hours available per month for the next 18 months for each line.

From the total numbers available for maintenance downtime, they will review the line history and decide the number of unplanned downtime hours to subtract from the overall total.

The remaining hours can be planned downtime for PM and AM.

Estimate Downtime Constraints

Here the planners review the maintenance plans for orders requiring downtime on their lines in the next 18 months. They enter the data for each month into the spreadsheet on the next page. Then they use the equipment/location rankings, data in the CMMS, and their knowledge to create downtime buckets and a critical path of orders within each bucket. Downtime "buckets" must be two hours in duration or longer.

Downtime buckets   Month _____ Line ____

Plan ##	Task List (Group, Counter #)	Pkge	Oper ##	Operation Description	Functional Location	Downtime (HRs) (SAP = Duration)	Date scheduled	Constraints

Example Downtime Buckets   **Month: March Line: 7**

Plan ##	Task List (Group, Counter #)	Pkge	Oper ##	Operation Description	Location/ Equipment	Downtime (HRs) (SAP = Duration)	Date scheduled	Constraints
1	01,01	100 OPH	10	Calibrate motor settings	CBDC-0001-0100-0030	2	16-Jun	Manager must be present
1	01,01	80 OPH	20	Clean motor	CBDC-0001-0100-0030	0.5	11-Jun	none
1	01,01	80 OPH	20	Clean motor	CBDC-0001-0100-0030	0.5	22-Jun	none
1	02,01	120 OPH	10	Lube motor	CBDC-0001-0100-0030	1	29-Jun	none
2	03,01	1W	10	Inspect motor alignment	CBDC-0001-0100-0030	0.3	5-Jun	none
2	03,01	1W	10	Inspect motor alignment	CBDC-0001-0100-0030	0.3	12-Jun	none
2	03,01	1W	10	Inspect motor alignment	CBDC-0001-0100-0030	0.3	19-Jun	none
2	03,01	1W	10	Inspect motor alignment	CBDC-0001-0100-0030	0.3	26-Jun	none
2	04,01	6w	10	Perform vibration analysis	CBDC-0001-0100	1.5	23-Jun	Contractor schedule for this date
3	Motor,01	4w	20	AMs for plant motors	various	0	wk of 6/8	none
3	Motor,02	4w	50	AMs for plant motors	various	0	wk of 6/22	none
4	05,01	26w	10	Overhaul	CBDC-0001-0100-0030	6	6-Jun	Must be on weekend, special test equipment required

Provide Production Planning Downtime Estimates

The maintenance planner uses the following spreadsheet to provide the production planners with the maintenance downtime requirements prior to the monthly PP/PM long-range meeting. They should list each critical path job and its constraints. Include dates, times, and downtime requirements.

Downtime Buckets   Month _____ Line _____

Operation Description	Location/Equipment	Downtime (HRs) (SAP = Duration)	Date scheduled	Constraints

Example Downtime Buckets   **Month: March Line: 7**

Operation Description	Location/Equipment	Downtime (HRs) (SAP = Duration)	Date scheduled	Constraints
Overhaul	CBDC-0001-0100-0030	6	6-Jun	Must be on weekend, special test equipment required
Clean motor	CBDC-0001-0100-0030	0.5	11-Jun	none
Calibrate motor settings	CBDC-0001-0100-0030	2	16-Jun	Manager must be present
Clean motor	CBDC-0001-0100-0030	0.5	22-Jun	none
Perform vibration analysis	CBDC-0001-0100	1.5	23-Jun	Contractor schedule for this date
Lube motor	CBDC-0001-0100-0030	1	29-Jun	none

Conduct monthly PP/PM meeting

The MCPP provides accurate data for planning inputs to PP planners. In addition, a meeting is held every month to review the MCPP with production personnel. This meeting incorporates inputs from previous planned work with reactive maintenance work, reliability requirements, production demand, and process improvements. When completed, the plan specifically prioritizes and plans maintenance work for the following month. This plan is used daily to track outstanding work and assign human resources as necessary to resolve pending work issues.

Production planner creates integrated production plan (MPS)

From the decisions made in the monthly meeting, the Production Planner enters the maintenance downtime requests and develops the long range production plans and the Master Production Schedule (MPS).

Maintenance planner fills in downtime windows with orders - Including constraints

Maintenance Planner fills in production intervals (downtime buckets) with the critical path work orders. Then adds work orders, which can be performed while critical path work is scheduled. In addition, a work order can be scheduled into planned changeovers if the resources are available. This schedule is roughed out on the spreadsheets until the orders are created.

Orders generated by CMMS

The CMMS will automatically generate orders from maintenance plans for the maintenance planner to review and approve.

Schedule work order

From their downtime spreadsheets with the critical path, the planner updates the newly created orders. If necessary, they change the order dates and times to match the pre-established downtime blocks. In addition, they schedule any reactive orders into the downtime blocks, adjusting their critical path if necessary.

The following is what it looks like conceptually in Excel.

Example Weekly Maintenance

Schedule

	2/5 I	2/5 II	2/5 III	2/6 I	2/6 II	2/6 III	2/7I	2/7 II	2/7 III	2/8 I	2/8 II	2/8 III	2/9 I	2/9 II	2/9 III
PM and AM Items	A-D	a 1700-1900	F-I	J-L	N-P	c,d,e,f,g,h 0200-0600	R,S	T-V	Z-AC	AD-AF	k,l,m 1530-1700	AH-AJ	o,p,q,s 0700-1000	AM-AP	AS-AV
Reactive Work		E	b,c 0000-0200	M	Q	i,j 0500-0600		W	X,Y	AG	n 1700-1800		AK-AL	AQ	AR
Emergencies															
Master Production Schedule - Down time Availability	None	1700-1900	0000-0200	None	None	0200-0600	None	None	None	None	1530-1800	None	0700-1000	None	None

I = 0700 - 1500

II = 1500 - 2300

III = 2300 - 0700

Capital letters are work orders to be completed while machines are running

Small letters are work orders to be completed during downtime

Reasons for downtime: production changeovers, outages, planned non-production time

Release Work Order

Once the order is created a request for the resources outlined in the order is made. However, they are not confirmed until the order is released. Once released, an order may have goods, labor, and services charged to it. An order should be rescheduled and released no later than 3 days after it is created.

Capacity Resolution

In the 90 to 30 days prior to the work being started, the planner can change/improve the contents of the order. They may add or remove resources, change downtime blocks, etc. In addition, they will need to use the capacity screens in your CMMS to verify the work center has the skills (suitability) and labor (available effort hours) to complete the work.

In many cases, production personnel will be needed to complete the maintenance tasks. Pooled capacity work centers may be needed to verify the maintenance work can be balanced with the production workload.

Changes may be made in this time period by production and maintenance planners as long as they do not violate the constraints of the work order. If so, the planners must jointly resolve any issues.

Dispatch Orders

At 30 days, firm zones are set and the order is ready to be dispatched. The planner enters the graphical planning table and dispatches each operation into the production schedule. At that point, the order's schedule cannot be changed without re-entering the graphical planning table.

Set firm zones

Firm maintenance planning zones are established 30 days in advance for each maintenance work order.

No changes are to be made in their schedule in the final seven days before any maintenance task unless caused by an emergency or safety event.

No changes are to be made in their schedule, seven to 30 days prior to the maintenance task unless agreed upon by maintenance and production personnel.

The goal is to use advance planning to establish a more flexible and more reliable integrated schedule which will reduce inventories and unplanned downtime.

Weekly Production meeting

Every week the Maintenance and Production Planners will meet to discuss their short and medium term scheduling plans. First, they will review the finite schedule for the next two weeks and confirm there are no scheduling or resource conflicts. Then, they review the following eleven weeks from a broader perspective. The goal is to resolve any near term issues and keep the plans current and executable.

The following slide illustrates the final timelines for the maintenance and production planning processes.

Some notes are:

- Average lead time for each part is 14 days - but will vary part by part
- Materials are received at the site five days before the planned work date.
- As soon as materials are delivered (at a minimum of 3 days before the work is to be performed) work can be moved forward for completion before its planned time and date. Otherwise the expectation is production will shut down on schedule to do maintenance.

Maintenance Planning and Scheduling Timeline

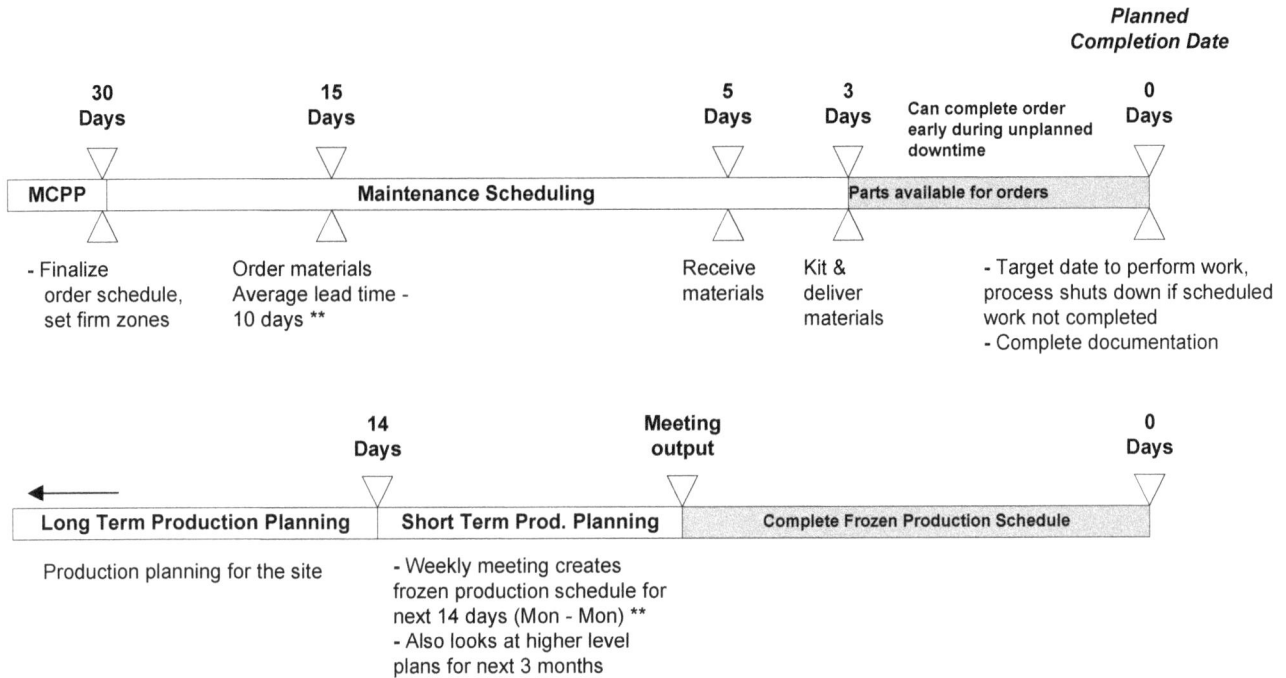

(c) 1998,
Steve Hampson

*Planned
Completion Date*

| 30 Days | 15 Days | 5 Days | 3 Days | | 0 Days |

Can complete order early during unplanned downtime

| MCPP | Maintenance Scheduling | Parts available for orders |

- Finalize order schedule, set firm zones

Order materials
Average lead time - 10 days **

Receive materials

Kit & deliver materials

- Target date to perform work, process shuts down if scheduled work not completed
- Complete documentation

| 14 Days | Meeting output | 0 Days |

| Long Term Production Planning | Short Term Prod. Planning | Complete Frozen Production Schedule |

Production planning for the site

- Weekly meeting creates frozen production schedule for next 14 days (Mon - Mon) **
- Also looks at higher level plans for next 3 months

** Will vary at each company

www.ingramcontent.com/pod-product-compliance
Lightning Source LLC
Chambersburg PA
CBHW081500200326
41518CB00015B/2330